THE
cookies
and
candy
COOKBOOK

SOUTHERN LIVING
PROGRESSIVE FARMER

Favorite Recipes Press © MCMLXXII
Library of Congress Catalog
Card Number 72-162992

contents

preface

You open a door . . . and are greeted with the aroma of freshly baked cookies or the sight of a pan filled with cooling candy. Then it all comes back. Christmas and the excitement of decorating a tree with cookies you baked yourself. The first time you prepared fudge — and it actually hardened. Yes, few things can bring back the warm memories evoked by homemade cookies and candy.

Southern Living homemakers know that these two foods are much more than just sweet tooth favorites; these women appreciate the traditions and memories involved with the preparation of cookies and candies. For that reason, cooks throughout the Southland have devoted much time and effort to developing and perfecting wonderful cookie and candy recipes.

Now the best of these recipes are shared with you in the pages of this Southern Living *Cookies and Candy Cookbook*. Filled cookies . . . bars . . . shaped cookies . . . even cookie recipes from foreign lands abound in these brightly-illustrated pages. There are even two special sections featuring cookies and candy recipes most suitable for small cooks.

This is a cookbook you will treasure for years to come and will depend on whenever you want to highlight an occasion as very special — and memorable. From our kitchens to yours, welcome to the wonderful world of cookies and candy — southern style!

Almond paste . . . . A paste made of finely ground, blanched almonds and cane sugar.

Bake . . . . To cook in an oven or oven-type appliance.

Baking powder . . . . A mixture of acid, carbonate and starch or flour which reacts with liquid and heat to produce gas that leavens batter and doughs.

Baking soda . . . . An alkali which reacts with an acid (e.g. sour milk or molasses) to form a gas that leavens batter and doughs.

Batter . . . . A mixture of flour, liquid, and other ingredients which may be poured or dropped.

glossary
COOKIE AND CANDY TERMS

Beat . . . . To make mixture smooth by the introduction of air with brisk whipping or stirring motions — using spoon or electric mixer.

Blanch . . . . To precook in boiling water or steam in order to inactivate enzymes and shrink food for canning, freezing, and drying, or removing skins.

Blend . . . . To mix two or more ingredients until smooth and uniform.

Brown sugar . . . . A soft sugar less refined than granulated sugar. There are two types, light and dark, and the dark is the stronger flavored.

Combine . . . . To intermix two or more ingredients until smooth; to blend.

Caramelize . . . . To melt sugar slowly over low heat until a brown color and characteristic flavor develops.

Chocolate . . . . A food prepared from ground, roasted cocoa beans and generally available for cooking purposes as semi-sweet, unsweetened, and German sweet chocolate.

Coats spoon . . . . Leaves a thin, even film on a metal spoon which is dipped into the cooking mixture, then removed and allowed to drain.

Cream . . . . To beat with spoon or electric mixer until mixture is soft and creamy. Usually applied to shortening and sugar.

Cut in . . . . To distribute solid fat in dry ingredients by chopping with pastry blender or with knives until finely divided.

Dough . . . . A mixture of moistened flour with other ingredients, thick enough to be handled or kneaded.

Fold . . . . To blend foods by cutting a spoon, spatula, or egg whip vertically down through the foods, turning it under and bringing it up vertically; repeating until mixing is complete.

Glaze . . . . A coating mixture applied to food which hardens or becomes firm and/or adds flavor and a glossy appearance.

Icing . . . . A thick mixture of sugar and other ingredients, either cooked or uncooked; frosting.

Kisses . . . . Small, meringue-type cookies dropped on a cookie sheet to form a peak and baked in a very low oven.

Knead . . . . To work dough by repeatedly stretching it with the hands, folding it over and pressing it with the knuckles or with the 'heel" of the hand.

Macaroons . . . . Cookies made from almond paste or powder, egg white, and sugar, usually with a distinct almond flavoring.

Meringue . . . . A mixture of stiffly beaten egg whites and sugar . . . baked until lightly browned.

Mocha . . . . A combination of coffee and chocolate flavors.

Sugar . . . . This term refers to beet or cane granulated white sugar. Types are: confectioners' or powdered sugar, granulated sugar, and superfine granulated sugar.

Whip . . . . To beat rapidly to incorporate air and produce expansion (e.g., heavy cream, egg whites) and a light, fluffy texture.

There is hardly a country which doesn't include in its cuisine recipes for the flavorful tidbits we call cookies. Certainly Americans — with their famous sweet tooth — are among the biggest fans of cookies. Southern homemakers, too, have capitalized on their families' love of cookies to develop many different recipes, the best of which are included in this cookbook.

All cookies, whatever their shape, flavor, or name, fall into one of five categories: drop, rolled, refrigerator, shaped, or bar. The way cookie dough is prepared for baking, its shape, and its texture all determine to which of these five groups a cookie belongs.

cookie knowledge

Drop cookies have slightly rounded tops and an irregular shape. Chocolate chip cookies are an example of a very popular drop cookie. All drop cookies are prepared from a dough which is mixed in one bowl and dropped onto a cookie sheet from two teaspoons. With one spoon a bit of dough about the size of a walnut is picked up. The other spoon is used to push it off onto the cookie sheet. Drop cookie dough is usually fairly soft and expands considerably during baking. For this reason, spoonfuls of dough should be placed about two inches apart on the cookie sheet. Because most drop cookie recipes yield several dozen cookies, they are favorites as cookie jar fillers. And almost all drop cookies are soft — making them very good travelers.

Rolled cookies are flat and crisp and are prepared from dough which has been rolled about one-quarter of an inch thick and cut into various shapes with thin-edged cookie cutters. Gingerbread men are typical of rolled cookies. The dough for preparing rolled cookies is stiffer and richer than drop cookie dough. Many cooks prefer to chill rolled cookie dough thoroughly and roll a small amount at a time. Such chilled dough holds its shape better during baking. After rolling out all the dough, and cutting out your cookies, bring the scraps together into a ball, and roll and cut one more time. Cookies prepared from the second rolling are less tender than those made from the first. Dough left over after the second rolling should be discarded. Because of their crisp texture, rolled cookies tend to break easily and are not suitable for mailing.

Refrigerator cookies are favorites of homemakers in a hurry. They are made from a very rich dough which is rolled into cylinders about two inches in diameter and chilled thoroughly. Cookies are then sliced off these firm rolls and baked. Refrigerator cookies are characteristically crisp and thin —

almost like rolled cookies in texture although not in shape. The cookie dough sold in the grocery stores' dairy section is essentially refrigerator cookie dough. Because of their crispness, refrigerator cookies break easily and so are not suitable for mailing.

Shaped cookies — like pressed ones such as spritz, are most often served at parties where their tiny, fanciful shapes are a delight to behold. The dough for pressed cookies is very rich with a high butter content and is so stiff it must be forced through the press. Chill the dough before putting it into a press as chilled dough holds its shape better. Many cooks also advise chilling or even partially freezing the shaped cookie dough on sheets before baking to minimize spreading and consequent loss of shape. Many pressed cookies are decorated with bits of candied fruit peel or halved maraschino cherries. Like drop cookies, these cookies travel well.

Shaped cookies — like peanut butter ones — are also prepared with a very stiff dough. But for these cookies the butter content is generally lower than it is for pressed cookie dough. The shaping is done by rolling bits of dough to form tiny bars or crescents or by flattening teaspoon-sized balls of dough with the bottom of a glass or the tines of a fork. Shaped cookie dough is easier to handle if it has been thoroughly chilled. If you are molding it with your hands, be sure they are well floured. Similarly, if your molding is done with the bottom of a glass or a fork, keep it well greased or dip it frequently in water. For extra-good sugar-topped shaped cookies, cover the bottom of the glass with a wet cloth napkin which has been wrung out. Dip it in sugar, and then mold the cookie by pressing a small ball of dough with the glass. The damp sugar adheres to the cookie and gives it a luscious sugar topping. And if you are going to dip your shaped cookies in sugar after baking, do it once immediately after the cookies have come out of the oven and once again after they have cooled.

Bar cookies, such as the ever-popular brownies, are quick-and-easy favorites. Made from a soft dough and baked in a shallow square or rectangular pan, they may have either a cake-like or fudgy texture, depending on the proportion of shortening to flour used. Some bar cookies are prepared in layers with coconut, chopped fruit, oatmeal, or cheese filling to provide flavor and texture contrast. And bar cookies, cut into large squares or rectangles are a marvelous dessert served just as they are or topped with ice cream and/or sauce! Bar cookies are good travelers but are best mailed in their baking pan. You might even consider not cutting them but leaving that fun for the happy recipient.

These are the five major varieties of cookies. Some are party-perfect, others serve double functions. Some mail well, others are best reserved for serving at home. And on the next two pages, you'll find valuable hints about choosing the right ingredients, mixing them properly, and baking all kinds of cookies — hints designed to make your cookies a delight to the eye as well as to the palate.

Before you actually begin the preparation of your cookie dough, you'll want to choose just the right recipe. Drop cookies and bars are the best for filling a cookie jar or mailing to someone far away. Shaped and pressed cookies are most often used as party refreshments although pressed cookies also make excellent cookie jar fillers. If your cookies are to be served to children or used as Christmas tree decorations, few tidbits are more delightful than rolled cookies. And, if you're in a hurry and need cookies in just a few minutes, slice a batch off the roll of refrigerator cookies you've prepared in advance.

INGREDIENTS

Once you've chosen your recipe, assemble your ingredients. For best results, ingredients should always be at room temperature. The basic ingredients of

general directions
FOR SUCCESSFUL COOKIES

any cookie recipe are sugar, flour, water or milk, eggs, shortening, and leavening. *Sugar* may be granulated or light brown; in some recipes for pressed or shaped cookies, confectioners' sugar may be specified. Measure confectioners' and granulated sugar by filling a measuring cup lightly to the specified measurement and leveling the top with a spatula or the back of a table knife. Brown sugar should be tightly packed into the measuring cup and should hold its shape when it is removed.

Recipes that specify *flour* usually mean all-purpose flour without any leavening agents added. Some flours are self-rising and are not suitable unless specifically called for in a recipe. Too much flour can make cookies tough and hard. For that reason, it should be sifted before measuring, then piled lightly into the cup and leveled along the top with the back of a knife or a spatula.

Eggs called for in recipes are usually large ones. If you must substitute egg sizes, allow three small or medium eggs for every two large ones. Eggs should be separated when cold but, like all other ingredients, should be allowed to come to room temperature before mixing.

Many recipes call for the addition of flavorings, chopped nuts, bits of candy, or coconut for flavor and texture variety. When chopping *nuts,* always use a knife or food chopper. If nuts are chopped in a food mill or grinder, they are reduced to a paste-like mass which may change the flavor or texture of your cookies. And do become an innovative cookie maker through the use of seasonings. Such spices as allspice, anise, cinnamon, cloves, ginger, mace, or nutmeg add much to the flavor of any cookie as do caraway, cardamom, poppy, or sesame seeds.

BAKING

The ideal cookie sheet is light-colored or teflon-coated metal with low sides, if any. Dark metal cookie sheets give cookies a heavy, dark crust. If you don't have a proper cookie sheet, turn a baking pan over and use the bottom. And grease a pan only when the recipe calls for it — many times greasing is unnecessary and alters the flavor of cookies disagreeably.

Place cookie sheets in the oven so that heat circulates around each one. They should not touch each other or the sides of the oven. And avoid placing one sheet over the other. When you do this, one batch invariably will have too-light tops and too-dark bottoms while the other will be too dark on top and too light on the bottom.

Most cookie recipes give a time range for baking, like 12 to 15 minutes per batch. The range is necessary because some people make bigger cookies than others. You should begin checking your cookies when the minimum cooking time specified has passed. Remove cookies from the oven as soon as they are a light brown and the middles have set. Cookies continue to bake for a few minutes after they have been taken out of the oven, and the middle will cook during that time.

Unless the recipe specifies otherwise, remove cookies from the pan immediately with a spatula. They should be cooled completely on a rack which permits air to circulate around them. Warm cookies should never be stored or piled atop one another.

STORING

Soft cookies should be stored in a container with a tight lid. They stay soft longer if an apple slice or orange section — well wrapped — is put into the jar with them. Crisp cookies should be kept in a tightly-sealed container. If they become soft, try setting them in a 300-degree oven for a few minutes before serving. This heat will crisp them again. Needless to say, soft and crisp cookies are never stored together!

Bar cookies may be stored in their baking pan. Just cover them with a piece of aluminum foil or plastic wrap sealed tightly around the edges.

MAILING

Of all the gifts which come from home, perhaps none is so treasured as a batch of homemade cookies. To prepare your delicious cookies for mailing wrap them in pairs, back to back. Line a sturdy box with foil and prepare a heavy bottom layer of shock-absorbent material. Popcorn, miniature marshmallows, or shredded paper are all good materials to pack cookies in. If you do use popcorn or marshmallows, be sure to include a note warning against eating them! Alternate layers of cookies and absorbent material to about one or two inches from the top. Finish with a thick layer of cushioning materials. Seal the box tightly and wrap with heavy paper. Tie it securely on the outside. When you are addressing the box, add the word "fragile" to ensure careful handling.

filled cookies

Filled cookies might well be called surprise cookies. A delicious cookie surrounds a flavorful fruit filling or frosting . . . or a marvelous filling is sandwiched between two flat cookies. Yes, filled cookies bring a delightful surprise as soon as you bite into them.

In this section, you'll find favorite filled cookie recipes of southern homemakers from Maryland to Texas, women who take pride in serving their families delicious foods. Some are bar cookies while others are rolled or drop cookies. But all share in common that wonderful element of excitement brought by a zesty filling. Even brownies – everyone's favorite bar cookies – take on new flavor when they're presented as Filled Brownies.

Fruit fillings are also featured in this section. Some recipes, like the one for Apricot Pinwheels, feature tart fruit flavors in harmony with a cookie. Others are designed for the sweeter tooth – Date Crescent Cookies is one of these. Citrus fruits come in for their share of attention as in the recipe for Pineapple Thumbprints – easy to prepare and so good, they'll literally vanish from the plate!

These are just a few of the exciting recipes waiting for you in the pages that follow. Every one is the home-tested favorite of the homemaker who shares it with you, and every one is just right for you to serve your family. Try these recipes today – you'll see what we mean!

13

APRICOT PINWHEELS

1/4 c. sugar	1 egg, beaten
1/2 tsp. salt	2 1/4 to 2 1/2 c. flour
1/4 c. margarine	1/3 c. apricot preserves
1/4 c. scalded milk	1/3 c. chopped pecans
1 pkg. dry yeast	Halved cherries
1/4 c. warm water	

Stir the sugar, salt and margarine into milk in a bowl and cool until lukewarm. Dissolve the yeast in warm water and stir in the egg and 1 cup flour. Add to sugar mixture and beat until smooth. Add enough remaining flour to make a soft dough and knead lightly on a floured surface. Place in the bowl and let rise for 1 hour. Roll out and cut into 2-inch squares. Combine the apricot preserves and pecans and place 1 teaspoon in center of each square of dough. Fold corners of dough to centers and top with a cherry half. Place on a greased cookie sheet. Bake at 350 degrees until golden brown.

Minnie Behr, Boerne, Texas

BANANA SQUARES

1 c. butter	Dash of salt
2 c. sugar	2 tsp. soda
4 eggs	4 tbsp. buttermilk
2 tsp. vanilla	4 lge. ripe mashed bananas
2 1/2 c. flour	

Cream the butter and sugar in a bowl. Add eggs, one at a time, beating well after each addition, then add vanilla. Sift dry ingredients together and add to creamed mixture alternately with buttermilk. Add the bananas and mix well. Place in 3 greased 11 x 7 1/4-inch pans. Bake at 325 degrees for 30 minutes.

Filling

1 c. (packed) brown sugar	1 stick butter, softened
1 can flaked coconut	4 tsp. evaporated milk

Mix all ingredients thoroughly and spread on hot baked mixture. Bake for 7 minutes longer and cut into squares.

Mrs. Nathaniel Hicks, Timberlake, North Carolina

BUTTER JEWEL COOKIES

3/4 lb. butter or margarine	1 1/2 tsp. vanilla
1 c. sugar	4 c. flour
2 egg yolks, beaten	Jelly
Pinch of salt	

Cream the butter and sugar in a bowl. Add the egg yolks, salt and vanilla and mix. Add flour and mix well. Roll into balls the size of a marble and place on ungreased baking sheet. Make an indentation in the tops with thumb and fill with jelly. Bake at 350 degrees for 15 minutes. 5 dozen.

Mrs. Richard Tatum, Laurinburg, North Carolina

CHOCOLATE-NUT MOSAICS

1 6-oz. package semisweet
   chocolate morsels
1 tbsp. shortening
1 c. finely chopped walnuts
1/2 c. sweetened condensed milk
1 1/2 tsp. vanilla
1 tsp. salt

1/4 c. soft butter or margarine
1/2 c. (firmly packed) brown
   sugar
1 egg yolk
1 c. sifted flour
1/4 tsp. baking powder

Melt the chocolate morsels and shortening over hot, not boiling, water. Remove from water and mix in the walnuts. Add the milk, 1 teaspoon vanilla and 1/4 teaspoon salt and blend thoroughly. Chill for about 30 minutes or until firm enough to handle. Turn onto waxed paper and shape into a roll 12 inches long. Wrap and chill. Cream the butter, brown sugar, egg yolk and remaining vanilla in a bowl. Sift the flour, remaining salt and baking powder together into creamed mixture and mix well. Form into a firm ball and roll out on waxed paper to 9 x 12-inch rectangle. Place chilled chocolate mixture along 12-inch edge and roll up to cover chocolate mixture. Wrap in waxed paper and chill until firm. Cut in 1/2-inch slices and place on ungreased cookie sheet. Bake in a 375-degree oven for 10 minutes. 2 dozen.

BUTTERSCOTCH-FILLED POINSETTIAS

1 c. soft butter	1/2 tsp. baking powder
1 c. sugar	1/4 tsp. salt
1 egg	Red food coloring
2 tsp. lemon juice	Butterscotch morsels
1 tsp. vanilla	Butterscotch Filling
3 c. sifted flour	

Cream the butter and sugar in a bowl and beat in egg, lemon juice and vanilla. Sift the flour, baking powder and salt together. Add to creamed mixture and blend until smooth. Add enough food coloring for a poinsettia red. Pack into cookie press with swirled flower plate and press onto ungreased cookie sheets about 1 inch apart. Press a butterscotch morsel in center of half the cookies. Bake in 375-degree oven for 12 to 15 minutes, then cool. Spread about 2 teaspoons Butterscotch Filling on smooth side of cookies without morsels and top with remaining cookies, morsel side up. About 3 dozen filled cookies.

Butterscotch Filling

1 6-oz. package butterscotch morsels	1 tsp. vanilla
1 3-oz. package cream cheese	2 1/2 c. sifted confectioners' sugar
1/4 tsp. salt	

Melt the butterscotch morsels over hot, not boiling, water, then remove from water. Mash the cream cheese with salt and vanilla and blend with melted morsels. Blend in confectioners' sugar.

CHEWY COOKIE SANDWICHES

2/3 c. shortening	1 tsp. vanilla
1 c. sugar	3 c. flour
2 eggs	3 tsp. baking powder
1/3 c. milk	1/2 tsp. salt

Cream the shortening and sugar in a bowl and stir in eggs, milk and vanilla. Sift dry ingredients together and add to creamed mixture gradually. Roll out thin on a floured surface and cut into rounds. Place half the rounds on greased cookie sheet.

Raisin Filling

1/2 c. sugar	1/2 c. water
1 tbsp. flour	1 c. raisins

Combine the sugar and flour in a saucepan and stir in the water and raisins. Cook until thick, stirring constantly. Place 1 teaspoon on each cookie on cookie sheet and cover with remaining cookies. Press edges together. Bake at 400 degrees for 10 to 15 minutes. 2 dozen.

Mrs. M. Nunnaly, Charleston, South Carolina

FILLED COTTAGE CHEESE COOKIES

3 c. sifted all-purpose flour	1 egg
1 tsp. baking powder	1 tsp. grated lemon rind
1 tsp. salt	1 tsp. vanilla
1/4 tsp. nutmeg	1 c. creamed cottage cheese
1 c. butter	1 c. thick raspberry preserves
1 c. sugar	

Sift the flour, baking powder, salt and nutmeg together. Cream the butter in a bowl. Add sugar gradually and cream well. Add egg, lemon rind, vanilla and cottage cheese and beat until smooth. Blend in flour mixture. Wrap in waxed paper and chill for several hours or overnight. Roll out to 1/8-inch thickness on lightly floured surface and cut with 2 1/2-inch round cookie cutter. Place half the rounds on greased baking sheet and place 1 teaspoon preserves in center of each round. Cut a small opening in center of remaining cookie rounds and place on preserves-topped cookie rounds. Press edges together with fork. Bake in 350-degree oven for 12 to 15 minutes or until lightly browned.

Terry Hartford, New Castle, Delaware

CREAM WAFERS

1 1/4 c. soft butter	3/4 c. powdered sugar
1/3 c. thick cream	1 egg yolk
2 c. sifted flour	1 tsp. vanilla
Sugar	

Place 1 cup butter, cream and flour in a bowl and mix well. Chill. Roll out 1/3 of the dough at a time on floured surface to 1/8-inch thickness. Cut with 1-inch cookie cutter. Sprinkle both sides with sugar and place on ungreased baking sheet. Prick with a fork. Bake at 375 degrees for 7 to 9 minutes or until light brown. Blend remaining butter with remaining ingredients. Spread between cookies in sandwich style.

Mrs. Clay Lowery, Pikeville, Kentucky

SURPRISE MOLASSES SANDWICH COOKIES

2 1/4 c. flour	1/2 c. shortening
1 tsp. soda	3/4 c. sugar
1/2 tsp. salt	2 eggs
1 tsp. cinnamon	2/3 c. molasses
1/2 tsp. ginger	1/2 c. milk

Sift the flour, soda, salt and spices together. Cream the shortening in a bowl. Add the sugar and cream until light and well blended. Add the eggs and beat well, then stir in the molasses. Add the flour mixture alternately with milk, mixing well after each addition. Drop by heaping teaspoonfuls onto greased baking sheet about 2 inches apart. Bake in 375-degree oven for 10 to 12 minutes, then cool.

Filling

1/2 c. butter or margarine	3 c. sifted confectioners' sugar
1/8 tsp. salt	1/4 c. molasses
1/2 tsp. ginger	2 tbsp. (about) milk

Cream the butter in a bowl. Add the salt, ginger and half the sugar gradually, blending well after each addition. Add remaining sugar alternately with molasses and milk, beating after each addition until smooth. Beat until right consistency to spread. Spread between 2 cookies to make sandwich cookies. 2 1/2 dozen.

FANCY SANDWICH COOKIES

3/4 c. butter	1 tsp. vanilla
1/4 c. (firmly packed) light brown sugar	2 c. sifted all-purpose flour
1/4 c. sugar	Vanilla Frosting
1 egg yolk	Pecan halves

Preheat oven to 350 degrees. Cream the butter in a mixing bowl. Add the sugars gradually and beat until light and fluffy. Beat in egg and vanilla and add flour gradually. Chill for ease in handling. Form into 2 rolls, each 7 inches long and 1 1/2 inches in diameter. Wrap in waxed paper and chill for several hours. Cut into 1/8-inch slices and place on baking sheets. Bake for 8 to 10 minutes. Remove to wire rack to cool. Place 2 cookies together with Vanilla Frosting. Place dollop of frosting on top of sandwich and top with pecan half.

Vanilla Frosting

1/4 c. butter	1/2 tsp. vanilla
1 3/4 c. confectioners' sugar	Food coloring
1 egg white	

Cream the butter in a small mixing bowl. Add sugar alternately with egg white, beating until light and fluffy. Blend in vanilla and desired amount of food coloring.

Photograph for this recipe on page 12.

DATE CRESCENT COOKIES

1 1/2 c. sifted cake flour	1 c. pitted dates, chopped
1/2 tsp. salt	1/2 c. chopped walnuts
Powdered sugar	1/3 c. sugar
1/3 c. butter or margarine	1/2 tsp. grated orange rind
2 to 3 tbsp. cold water	2 tbsp. orange juice

Sift the flour, salt and 2 tablespoons powdered sugar together into a bowl. Cut in butter until mixture resembles coarse meal. Sprinkle with water and toss lightly with fork until ingredients hold together. Form into a ball and roll out thin on floured board. Cut into 3-inch squares. Combine remaining ingredients and mix well. Place 1 teaspoon on each square and bring edges together to form a triangle. Seal with tines of fork and place on greased baking sheet. Curve slightly. Bake at 375 degrees for about 20 minutes. Roll in powdered sugar while warm. 2 dozen.

Mrs. Dorothy Morris, Ooltewah, Tennessee

DATE AND NUT-FILLED COOKIES

1 lb. margarine	1 c. chopped nuts
2 8-oz. packages cream cheese	1/2 c. sugar
3 c. flour	1/2 c. water
1 lb. chopped dates	

Mix first 3 ingredients in a bowl and chill overnight. Roll out very thin on a floured surface and cut with round cutter. Mix remaining ingredients in a saucepan and cook until thick. Cool. Place 1 teaspoon on each cookie round. Fold over and press ends together. Place on a cookie sheet. Bake at 375 degrees for 20 to 25 minutes.

Mrs. T. W. Browning, Knoxville, Tennessee

EASY MOLASSES COOKIES

1/2 c. shortening	1 tsp. cinnamon
1 c. sugar	2 tsp. ginger
1 egg	2 tsp. soda
1 c. molasses	1 c. boiling water
4 c. flour	1/4 lb. butter
1/2 tsp. salt	3 to 4 c. powdered sugar
1 tsp. nutmeg	1 tsp. vanilla
1 tsp. cloves	2 tbsp. milk

Cream the shortening in a bowl. Add sugar and egg and beat well. Add the molasses and mix. Sift dry ingredients together and add to molasses mixture alternately with water. Drop by teaspoonfuls on greased cookie sheet. Bake at 400 degrees for 10 minutes and cool. Blend remaining ingredients and place on half the cookies. Top with remaining cookies in sandwich style.

Mrs. Belle Cox, Charleston, West Virginia

FILLED BROWNIES

1/3 c. shortening	1/2 tsp. vanilla
1 c. sugar	2 sq. melted chocolate
1/4 tsp. salt	2/3 c. sifted flour
2 eggs	1/2 c. chopped nuts

Cream the shortening, sugar, salt, eggs and vanilla in a bowl. Stir in remaining ingredients and mix well. Pour into waxed paper-lined and greased jelly roll pan. Bake at 350 degrees for 15 minutes. Remove from pan and peel off waxed paper. Cut in half.

Filling

1 tbsp. hot milk	1/4 tsp. almond extract
1 tsp. shortening	1 c. powdered sugar

Mix all ingredients and spread on half the baked mixture. Place remaining baked mixture on top and cut into small squares.

Mrs. F. A. Boles, Pine Bluff, Arkansas

EASY-FILLED DATE COOKIES

1 c. soft shortening	1 tsp. soda
2 c. (packed) brown sugar	1/8 tsp. cinnamon
2 eggs	2 c. chopped dates
1/2 c. buttermilk or sour milk	3/4 c. sugar
1 tsp. vanilla	3/4 c. water
3 1/2 c. sifted flour	1/2 c. chopped nuts
1 tsp. salt	

Cream the shortening and brown sugar in a bowl. Add eggs and mix well. Mix the buttermilk and vanilla. Sift the flour, salt, soda and cinnamon together and add to creamed mixture alternately with buttermilk mixture. Drop 2/3 of the dough from teaspoon onto ungreased cookie sheet. Mix the dates, sugar and water in a saucepan and cook, stirring constantly, until thickened. Add nuts and cool. Place 1/2 teaspoon date filling on each unbaked cookie and cover with 1/2 teaspoon remaining dough. Bake at 400 degrees for 10 to 12 minutes or until lightly browned. 5 dozen.

Annette Parker, Brandon, Mississippi

FRUIT-FILLED COOKIES

1 1/2 c. sugar	1 tsp. salt
1 c. shortening	1 tsp. soda
2 eggs	2 tsp. baking powder
1 c. buttermilk	1/2 lb. raisins
1 tsp. vanilla	1/2 lb. figs
1 tsp. lemon flavoring	1/2 lb. pitted dates
3 c. flour	1/2 c. water

Blend the sugar and shortening in a bowl. Add eggs, buttermilk and flavorings and mix well. Sift dry ingredients together and stir into sugar mixture. Chill. Grind the fruits and place in a saucepan. Add the water and cook for 15 minutes, stirring frequently. Cool. Roll out the dough on a floured surface and cut with a cookie cutter. Place 1 spoon filling on half the cookies and cover with remaining cookies. Seal edge. Place on a greased cookie sheet. Bake at 375 degrees for 10 to 15 minutes.

Mrs. E. D. McKeown, Greensboro, North Carolina

FILLED BUTTER COOKIES

1 lb. butter or margarine	Powdered sugar
4 eggs, beaten	Nut filling
4 c. sifted flour	Apricot filling
4 tsp. baking powder	Prune filling
4 tbsp. sour milk	

Cream the butter in a bowl. Add the eggs and mix well. Mix the flour and baking powder and add to butter mixture alternately with milk. Knead for about 5 minutes on a powdered sugar-coated surface. Divide into 3 parts. Roll out, 1 part at a time, to 1/8-inch thickness on powdered sugar-coated surface. Cut into 2-inch squares. Place 1/4 teaspoon filling on each square and fold. Seal edges. Place on greased cookie sheet. Bake for 20 minutes at 350 degrees. Cool and sprinkle with powdered sugar.

Mrs. W. M. Petrie, Baton Rouge, Louisiana

CRISSCROSS COOKIES

1 1/2 c. chopped dates	2 eggs
1/2 c. chopped walnuts	3 tbsp. cream or sour cream
1 3/4 c. sugar	1 tsp. vanilla
1/2 c. water	1/2 tsp. lemon extract
1 tbsp. light corn syrup	3 c. sifted flour
1 tsp. vinegar	1/2 tsp. soda
Salt	Powdered sugar
1 c. mixed shortening and butter	

Combine the dates, walnuts, 1/4 cup sugar, water, corn syrup, vinegar and dash of salt in a saucepan and cook for 2 to 3 minutes, stirring constantly. Remove from heat and cool. Cream the shortening mixture in a bowl and add remaining sugar gradually, creaming until fluffy. Beat in the eggs, one at a time, then stir in the cream and flavorings. Sift the flour with soda and 1/2 teaspoon salt. Add to creamed mixture and mix well. Chill thoroughly. Roll out, 1/4 of the dough at a time, to 1/8-inch thickness on powdered sugar-coated canvas or board. Cut in 2 1/2-inch circles or in shape of hearts, diamonds, spades, and clubs and place 1 inch apart on ungreased cookie sheet. Spread date filling on each cookie, leaving 1/4-inch margin. Cut narrow strips from rolled-out dough. Crisscross over filling and press ends to cookie edges lightly. Trim, if necessary. Bake at 375 degrees for 10 to 12 minutes or until lightly browned. 4-5 dozen.

PEANUT SURPRISE COOKIES

2/3 c. shortening	1 c. sifted all-purpose flour
1/3 c. (packed) light brown sugar	1/2 tsp. baking powder
2 eggs, separated	1/2 c. peanut butter
1/2 tsp. almond extract	1 1/3 c. chopped salted peanuts

Cream the shortening and sugar in a bowl. Add egg yolks and beat until light and fluffy. Add the almond extract. Sift the flour with baking powder and stir into creamed mixture. Chill. Shape into 24 balls and flatten each on lightly floured board. Place 1 teaspoon peanut butter in the center of each and wrap the dough around peanut butter. Roll in slightly beaten egg whites, then in peanuts. Place on lightly greased baking sheet. Bake at 350 degrees for 12 to 15 minutes.

Mrs. W. C. Ellis, Mobile, Alabama

RAISIN-FILLED COOKIES

1 c. sugar	1 tsp. soda
1 c. (packed) brown sugar	1 tbsp. sour milk
5 c. flour	3 eggs, well beaten
1/2 tsp. nutmeg	2 tsp. vanilla
1 tsp. baking powder	Filling
1 c. mixed lard and butter	

Mix first 5 ingredients in a bowl and cut in the lard mixture. Dissolve the soda in sour milk and add to sugar mixture. Add the eggs and vanilla and mix well. Roll very thin on a floured surface and cut into desired shapes. Place 1 teaspoon Filling on half the cookies. Place remaining cookies on top and seal edges. Place on a greased cookie sheet. Bake at 375 degrees for 12 to 15 minutes.

Filling

1 1/2 c. ground raisins	2 tbsp. cornstarch
1 c. (packed) brown sugar	1/2 tsp. nutmeg
1 c. water	1 tsp. vanilla

Combine all ingredients except vanilla in a saucepan and cook until thick. Add the vanilla and cool.

Martha Mongold, Brushy Run, West Virginia

RAISIN MUMBLES

2 1/2 c. raisins	1 c. (packed) brown sugar
1/2 c. sugar	1 3/4 c. sifted flour
2 tbsp. cornstarch	1/2 tsp. salt
3/4 c. water	1/2 tsp. soda
3 tbsp. lemon juice	1 1/2 c. rolled oats
3/4 c. soft butter	

Combine first 5 ingredients in a saucepan and cook over low heat, stirring constantly, until thick. Cool. Cream the butter and brown sugar in a bowl. Add remaining ingredients and mix well. Press half the mixture into 9 x 13-inch pan. Spread with raisin mixture and press remaining oats mixture on top. Bake at 400 degrees for 20 to 30 minutes and cool. Cut in squares.

Mrs. S. W. Carden, Enid, Oklahoma

PINEAPPLE THUMBPRINTS

1 sm. can crushed pineapple	1/4 c. sugar
1 1/2 c. sifted flour	1 tsp. vanilla
1 tsp. soda	1 1/2 c. crushed corn flakes
3/4 c. butter or margarine	1/2 c. chopped walnuts (opt.)
3/4 c. (packed) brown sugar	

Drain the pineapple and reserve 1 tablespoon syrup. Sift flour and soda together. Cream the butter and sugars in a bowl. Add the flour mixture, vanilla and reserved syrup and mix well. Stir in corn flakes and shape into 1-inch balls. Place 2 1/2 inches apart on cookie sheet. Make an indentation in each with thumb and fill with crushed pineapple. Top with walnuts. Bake at 350 degrees for 18 minutes.

Evelyn Jean Maez, Las Vegas, New Mexico

SURPRISE COOKIES

1/2 c. shortening	2 1/2 c. flour
1 c. sugar	1 tsp. soda
2 eggs	2 tsp. baking powder
1/2 tsp. vanilla	1/2 tsp. salt
1/2 c. sour milk	Fig Filling

Cream the shortening and sugar in a bowl. Add the eggs, vanilla and milk and mix well. Sift dry ingredients together and stir into creamed mixture. Roll out wafer thin on floured surface and cut in desired shapes. Place 1 teaspoon Fig Filling on half the cookies. Place remaining cookies on top and press edges together. Place on cookie sheet. Bake at 425 degrees until brown.

Fig Filling

1 c. chopped dried figs	1/2 c. chopped nuts
1 c. water	1 tsp. flour
1/2 c. sugar or corn syrup	

Combine all ingredients in a saucepan and cook until thick. Cool.

Mrs. Earl D. Clark, Kissimmee, Florida

SPLIT SECOND

3/4 c. butter or margarine	2 c. flour
2/3 c. sugar	1/2 tsp. baking powder
1 egg, well beaten	1/3 c. currant jelly
2 tsp. vanilla	

Cream the butter and sugar in a bowl. Add egg and vanilla and mix. Sift the flour with baking powder and stir into creamed mixture. Place on floured board and knead lightly. Divide into 4 parts. Shape each part into a roll 13 inches long and 3/4 inch thick and place 4 inches apart on 2 ungreased baking sheets. Make a lengthwise depression 1/4 inch deep down the center of each roll and fill with jelly. Bake at 325 degrees for 15 minutes or until golden brown. Cut into diagonal slices while warm and remove to rack to cool.

Mrs. Steve York, Beaufort, South Carolina

GINGER-PEACH COOKIES

1 1-lb. 13-oz. can cling peach slices	1 c. shortening
1/2 c. (packed) brown sugar	2 c. sugar
3 tbsp. cornstarch	2 eggs
3/4 tsp. salt	1/2 c. sour cream
1/4 tsp. ground ginger	1/2 tsp. almond extract
1 tbsp. butter or margarine	4 c. sifted flour
1/2 tsp. grated lemon rind	1 tsp. soda

Drain the peaches and reserve 1/2 cup syrup. Chop the peaches fine. Combine the brown sugar, cornstarch, 1/4 teaspoon salt, ginger, butter, lemon rind and reserved syrup in a saucepan. Stir in the peaches and cook until thickened. Cool. Cream the shortening and sugar in a bowl and beat in the eggs, sour cream and almond extract. Sift flour, soda and remaining salt together and stir into creamed mixture. Divide into 2 parts. Roll 1 part out on floured board into 18 x 12-inch rectangle and cut into 24 squares. Place on lightly greased cookie sheet and center each square with 1 heaping teaspoon peach mixture. Roll out remaining dough into 18 x 12-inch rectangle and cut into 24 squares. Score centers with an X and turn back cut edges. Place over peach-filled squares and press outside edges together gently. Bake in 375-degree oven for 12 to 15 minutes.

THIMBLE COOKIES

2 1/4 c. sifted flour	2 eggs
1 1/2 tsp. baking powder	1/2 tsp. vanilla
1/2 tsp. salt	1 tbsp. milk
3/4 c. margarine	2 tbsp. water
2/3 c. (firmly packed) brown	1 1/2 c. finely chopped nuts
sugar	Jam or jelly
1/3 c. dark corn syrup	

Sift the flour, baking powder and salt together and set aside. Blend the margarine and sugar in a mixing bowl and blend in the corn syrup. Add 1 egg, then 1 egg yolk, beating well after each addition, and stir in the vanilla. Add sifted ingredients alternately with the milk and chill for 4 hours or overnight or until firm enough to handle. Shape into 1-inch balls. Beat the egg white slightly and combine with water. Dip balls into egg white mixture, then roll in nuts. Place about 1 inch apart on lightly greased cookie sheet. Dough will be soft. Bake in 375-degree oven for 5 minutes and remove from oven. Make depression in top of each cookie with a thimble and fill with about 1/4 teaspoon jam. Return to oven and bake for about 10 minutes longer. Remove from cookie sheet immediately and cool on wire rack. About 6 dozen.

TIP-TOPS

1/2 c. shortening	2 1/2 tsp. baking powder
2 c. sugar	1/2 c. cocoa
2 eggs	1 c. boiling water
4 1/2 c. flour	1 c. sour milk
1/2 tsp. salt	1 tsp. vanilla
2 tsp. soda	

Cream the shortening and sugar in a bowl and stir in the eggs. Sift dry ingredients together. Mix remaining ingredients and add to creamed mixture alternately with sifted ingredients. Roll out on a floured surface and cut into desired shapes. Place on a greased cookie sheet. Bake at 350 degrees for 10 minutes.

Filling

1 c. milk	1 c. sugar
5 tbsp. flour	1/2 tsp. salt
1 c. shortening	1 tsp. vanilla

Mix the milk and flour in a saucepan and cook until thick. Cool. Combine remaining ingredients in a bowl. Add flour mixture slowly and beat until light and fluffy. Spread on half the cookies and cover with remaining cookies.

Mrs. Ezra Steele, Radford, Virginia

WHOOPIE PIE COOKIES

1 c. shortening	1 1/2 tsp. salt
1 c. sugar	1 c. sour milk
2 eggs, beaten	2 tsp. soda
5 c. flour	1 c. hot water
3/4 c. cocoa	

Cream the shortening and sugar in a bowl and stir in the eggs. Sift dry ingredients together and add to creamed mixture alternately with sour milk. Combine the soda and hot water and stir into flour mixture. Drop from spoon onto greased cookie sheet. Bake at 400 degrees for 10 to 15 minutes.

Filling

2 egg whites	4 tbsp. milk
2 tsp. vanilla	1 c. shortening
4 c. powdered sugar	

Beat the egg whites, vanilla, 2 cups powdered sugar in a bowl until stiff, adding milk, if needed. Cream remaining powdered sugar and shortening in a bowl and add to egg white mixture gradually. Spread on half the cookies and cover with remaining cookies.

Mrs. Charles Clifford, Pikeville, Kentucky

THUMBPRINT COOKIES

1/2 c. soft shortening	1/4 tsp. salt
1/4 c. brown sugar	3/4 c. finely chopped nuts
1 egg, separated	Jelly or tinted powdered
1/2 tsp. vanilla	sugar
1 c. sifted flour	

Cream the shortening and sugar in a bowl and stir in the egg yolk and vanilla. Sift dry ingredients together and stir into creamed mixture. Roll into 1-inch balls and dip in slightly beaten egg white. Roll in nuts and place 1 inch apart on ungreased baking sheet. Press thumb into center of each. Bake at 375 degrees for 10 to 12 minutes or until brown. Cool. Place jelly in thumbprints.

Jimmie McGuire, Davis, Oklahoma

dessert bars & squares

Cookies are wonderfully versatile! *Southern Living* homemakers know that a batch of bar cookies can be transformed into an elegant dessert . . . they simply cut the squares about twice as large as usual and top them with ice cream and fudge sauce. What a marvelous way to perk up an ordinary supper menu!

There are many bar cookies which can do double duty as cookies and dessert treats, and in the pages that follow, you'll meet some of them. Some are variations on an all-time favorite bar cookie – the brownie. For your next special luncheon or tea, offer your guests elegant Brownie Petit Fours. And if yours is a family that loves both chocolate and cheesecake, Cream Cheese Brownies were made for you! Watch for compliments when you cap a meal with these rich tidbits.

Traditional fruit favorites play their roles too. Recipes for Date Delight Bars, Mincemeat Mixup Bars, and many other fruity desserts give you a wide variety of richly flavorful, chewy bars. And for a change of pace, offer your family Butterscotch Brickle Bars, smothered with whipped topping.

The next time you're looking for a dessert in a hurry, turn to this section. In it you'll find recipes certain to bring you heartwarming compliments – and very special taste treats as well!

ENGLISH TOFFEE BARS

1 c. butter
1 c. sugar
1 egg, separated
2 c. sifted all-purpose
    flour

1 tsp. cinnamon
1 c. chopped pecans
2 2-oz. squares semisweet
    chocolate, melted

Preheat oven to 275 degrees. Cream the butter in a mixing bowl. Add sugar gradually and beat until light and fluffy. Beat in the egg yolk. Sift flour and cinnamon together and add to creamed mixture gradually. Press evenly into a greased 15 1/2 x 10 1/2 x 1-inch jelly roll pan. Brush top with slightly beaten egg white. Sprinkle with pecans and press lightly into dough. Bake for 1 hour. Cut into 1 1/2-inch squares or diamonds while hot and drizzle with melted chocolate. Cool on wire rack. 5-6 dozen.

Photograph for this recipe on page 49.

APRICOT-NUT BARS

4 eggs, well beaten
2 1/2 c. (firmly packed) light
    brown sugar
1 tall can evaporated milk
2 tbsp. lemon juice
2 1/2 c. sifted flour
1 1/2 tsp. soda

1 tsp. cinnamon
1/2 tsp. salt
1 c. chopped dried apricots
1 c. chopped walnuts
1 c. flaked coconut
Confectioners' sugar

Preheat oven to 350 degrees. Combine the eggs, brown sugar, evaporated milk and lemon juice in a large mixing bowl. Sift flour, soda, cinnamon and salt together and add all at once to egg mixture. Stir just until blended. Fold in the apricots, walnuts and coconut. Place in 2 well-greased 15 1/2 x 10 1/2 x 1-inch jelly roll pans. Bake for 20 minutes. Cool in pans and sprinkle lightly with confectioners' sugar. Cut into bars and remove from pans. Store in covered container. 5 dozen.

Photograph for this recipe on page 28.

BUTTERSCOTCH BRICKLE BARS

1 1/2 c. sifted flour
3/4 c. (packed) brown sugar
1/2 c. soft butter or margarine
1/2 tsp. salt

1 6-oz. package butterscotch bits
1/4 c. corn syrup
2 tbsp. vegetable shortening
2 c. coarsely chopped walnuts

Combine the flour, brown sugar, butter and 1/4 teaspoon salt and blend until crumbly. Press into a lightly greased 9 x 13 x 2-inch pan. Bake for 10 minutes at 375 degrees. Combine the butterscotch bits, corn syrup, shortening, 1 tablespoon water and the remaining salt in the top of a double boiler. Stir over hot but not boiling water until smooth and melted. Blend in the walnuts and spoon over baked layer, spreading evenly. Bake for 8 minutes longer. Cut into 24 bars while still warm.

Emily Brown, San Antonio, Texas

BLACK AND WHITE BARS

2 eggs	1/4 tsp. salt
1 c. sugar	2/3 c. coconut
1/3 c. melted butter	1/2 tsp. almond extract
2/3 c. flour	2 sq. chocolate, melted
3/4 tsp. baking powder	

Beat the eggs and sugar together and blend in the butter. Sift the flour, baking powder and salt together and stir into the egg mixture. Mix the coconut and almond extract into one-third of the batter. Blend the chocolate in the remaining batter. Spread the chocolate batter into a greased 8 x 8 x 2-inch pan and spread the coconut batter over the top. Bake at 350 degrees for 25 to 30 minutes. Cool and cut into bars.

Helen Mullikin, Hampton, South Carolina

DELTA BARS

1/2 c. butter	1/4 tsp. salt
1 c. sugar	1 tsp. vanilla
2 eggs, separated	1/2 c. brown sugar
1 c. sifted flour	1 c. chopped pecans
1/2 tsp. baking powder	

Cream the butter and sugar until fluffy, then add the egg yolks and beat well. Sift the flour, baking powder and salt together and add to the butter mixture gradually, beating constantly. Stir in the vanilla. Press the dough into an 8 1/2 x 13 1/2 x 1 1/2-inch pan. Beat the egg whites until stiff and fold in the brown sugar and pecans. Spread over the dough. Bake at 325 degrees for 30 to 35 minutes. Cool in pan and cut into bars.

Miss Bessie Boyd, Huntsville, Texas

DATE DELIGHT BARS

3 eggs	1/4 tsp. vanilla
3/4 c. brown sugar	1/2 c. whole wheat flour
1/2 lb. chopped dates	1 1/2 tsp. baking powder
1 c. chopped pecans	

Beat the eggs well and add the brown sugar, beating well. Stir in the dates, pecans and vanilla. Sift the flour and baking powder into the egg mixture and mix well. Spread in an ungreased 7 x 11 x 1 1/2-inch cake pan. Bake at 350 degrees for 45 minutes or until done. Cool slightly and cut into bars.

Esta Wiseman, Houston, Texas

PEANUT BUTTERSCOTCH BARS

1/2 c. peanut oil	1/4 tsp. baking powder
1 c. (packed) dark brown sugar	2 to 3 tbsp. milk
1 egg	1/2 c. chopped salted peanuts
1 tsp. vanilla	Lemon Confectioners' Sugar Glaze
2 c. sifted flour	

Place the peanut oil, brown sugar, egg and vanilla in a mixing bowl and stir until blended. Sift the flour with baking powder and stir into peanut oil mixture, adding enough milk to make dough medium-stiff. Stir in the peanuts and press into a greased 9-inch square baking pan. Bake at 350 degrees for 25 to 30 minutes or until lightly browned around edges. Remove from oven and spread Lemon-Confectioners' Sugar Glaze over the top while hot. Cool and cut into bars.

Lemon-Confectioners' Sugar Glaze

1 c. sifted confectioners' sugar	1/4 tsp. lemon extract
2 to 3 tbsp. milk	

Blend confectioners' sugar with milk. Mixture should be thin. Stir in the lemon extract. One-half teaspoon grated lemon rind may be substituted for lemon extract.

CARAMEL-COCONUT BARS

2 eggs
1 c. sugar
1 c. flour
1 tsp. baking powder

1/2 c. milk, scalded
2 tbsp. butter
1 tsp. vanilla

Beat the eggs and the sugar together and add the flour and baking powder. Combine the milk and butter and stir until butter is melted. Add to the egg mixture, then stir in the vanilla and spread in a square cake pan. Bake at 375 degrees for 25 minutes.

Icing

7 tbsp. brown sugar
3 tbsp. butter

2 tbsp. milk
1 pkg. coconut

Combine the brown sugar, butter and milk in a saucepan and heat, stirring until melted. Add the coconut and bring to a boil. Spread over warm cake and brown under broiler. Cut into bars. 1 dozen.

Mrs. Roy W. Paxton, Tenaha, Texas

CHOCOLATE RIPPLE BARS

1 c. butter
2 c. sugar
4 eggs
2 sq. unsweetened chocolate,
   melted

2 tsp. vanilla
1 1/2 c. sifted flour
1 tsp. baking powder
1 tsp. salt
1 c. chopped pecans

Cream the butter and sugar and add the eggs. Blend in the chocolate and vanilla. Add dry ingredients to creamed mixture and mix well. Stir in the pecans and spread in a lightly greased and floured 15 1/2 x 10 1/2 x 1-inch pan. Bake at 350 degrees for 30 minutes, then cool.

Frosting

1/3 c. butter
Sifted confectioners' sugar
3 tbsp. cream
1/2 tsp. vanilla

1 sq. unsweetened chocolate,
   melted
1 tbsp. melted butter

Melt the butter and blend in 3 cups confectioners' sugar, cream and vanilla. Spread on the baked mixture. Combine the chocolate, melted butter and 1 tablespoon confectioners' sugar and drizzle over the frosting. Cut into bars when icing has hardened.

Mrs. Frank Humphrey, Burgaw, North Carolina

MINCEMEAT MIX-UP BARS

1 1/2 c. flour	2 eggs
1/2 tsp. salt	3/4 c. mincemeat
1/2 tsp. cinnamon	1/2 c. crushed pineapple
1/4 tsp. soda	1/2 c. chopped nuts
3/4 c. sugar	2 c. powdered sugar
1/4 c. shortening	2 to 3 tbsp. pineapple juice

Sift the flour, salt, cinnamon and soda together. Cream the sugar and shortening and add the eggs, one at a time, beating well after each addition. Stir in the mincemeat, pineapple and nuts, mixing well. Add the dry ingredients and mix well. Spread the mixture in a 15 1/2 x 10 1/2 x 1-inch pan. Bake at 350 degrees for 20 to 30 minutes. Combine powdered sugar and pineapple juice for glaze and spread over hot mixture. Cut into bars. 4 dozen.

Mrs. Albert Lee, Silver Spring, Maryland

MOLASSES-COFFEE COOKIES

1 1/2 c. sifted flour	1/2 c. shortening
1 1/2 tsp. baking powder	1/2 c. sugar
3/4 tsp. salt	1 egg, beaten
1/4 tsp. soda	1/2 c. molasses
1 tsp. cinnamon	1/3 c. hot strong coffee
1/2 tsp. cloves	

Sift the flour, baking powder, salt, soda, cinnamon and cloves together. Cream the shortening and add sugar slowly, creaming together until light and fluffy. Blend in the egg and molasses, then add the flour mixture and hot coffee alternately. Turn the batter into a 9 x 13-inch greased pan. Bake at 350 degrees for 25 minutes or until done. Cool in pan.

Coffee Icing

1 2/3 c. confectioners' sugar	2 tbsp. hot strong coffee
1/4 c. soft margarine	3/4 c. finely chopped pecans
1/8 tsp. salt	

Sift the confectioners' sugar and beat into the margarine. Add the salt and coffee and beat for 2 or 3 minutes or until of spreading consistency. Spread on the baked mixture and press the pecans into the icing. Cut into bars. About 4 dozen bars.

Mrs. Arthur L. Williams, Macon, Georgia

ORANGE BARS

1 tsp. soda	2 c. sugar
1 c. sour cream or sour milk	2 eggs
1 c. shortening	Juice and grated rind of 2 oranges

4 1/2 c. flour, sifted	1 tsp. salt
2 tsp. baking powder	1 tsp. vanilla

Add the soda to the sour cream. Cream the shortening and sugar and add the eggs, orange juice and rind. Sift the flour, baking powder and salt together and add to creamed mixture alternately with sour cream mixture. Stir in the vanilla. Spread in 2 oblong baking pans. Bake at 350 degrees for 25 minutes or until done.

Icing

1 1/2 c. powdered sugar	2 tbsp. orange juice
3 tbsp. melted butter	1 tbsp. grated orange rind

Combine all the ingredients and spread over the baked mixture. Cool and cut into bars.

Mrs. Ronald Ekberg, Babson Park, Florida

CALIFORNIA SATIN SQUARES

1/2 c. butter or margarine	1/2 tsp. salt
1 c. (firmly packed) brown sugar	1 c. evaporated milk
2 eggs	1 12-oz. package semisweet chocolate morsels
2 tsp. vanilla	1/2 c. chopped California walnuts
2 c. sifted all-purpose flour	
1 tsp. baking powder	

Cream the butter and brown sugar in a bowl, then beat in eggs and vanilla. Sift flour, baking powder and salt together and add to creamed mixture alternately with evaporated milk. Stir in 1 cup chocolate morsels and spread in 2 ungreased 9-inch square pans. Bake in 350-degree oven for 25 minutes. Sprinkle with remaining chocolate morsels immediately and let stand until chocolate softens. Spread evenly over tops and sprinkle with walnuts. Cool and cut into 1 1/2-inch squares. 6 dozen.

Photograph for this recipe on page 5.

BROWNIE PETITS FOURS

2 c. sugar	1 tbsp. vanilla
1/2 c. cocoa	1 1/4 c. flour
1 stick butter or margarine, melted	Chocolate icing
4 lge. eggs	Pecan halves

Mix the sugar and cocoa together and add the melted butter. Add the eggs, one at a time, beating after each addition. Add the vanilla and flour and mix well. Turn into a greased 9 x 13-inch pan. Bake for 20 minutes at 350 degrees. Cut into squares while hot. Cool. Ice top and sides with chocolate icing and place a pecan half on top. 30 squares.

Mrs. Hugh Harrell, Ahoskie, North Carolina

CREAM CHEESE BROWNIES

3/4 c. sifted flour	2 eggs
1/2 tsp. baking powder	1 c. sugar
1/2 tsp. salt	1 tsp. vanilla
5 tbsp. cocoa	1/2 c. chopped pecans
1/2 c. shortening, softened	

Sift the flour, baking powder, salt and cocoa together. Add the shortening, eggs, sugar and vanilla and mix with mixer at low speed for 30 seconds. Scrape sides of bowl and beater, then beat at medium speed for 1 minute. Add the pecans and continue beating at medium speed for 1 minute longer. Pour into a greased 8 x 8 x 2-inch pan. Bake at 350 degrees for about 35 minutes.

Icing

2 3-oz. packages cream cheese, softened	1 1/2 tbsp. milk
3/4 c. sugar	1 tsp. vanilla

Combine all the ingredients and mix thoroughly with mixer. Spread over brownies. Cut in squares while warm.

Mrs. Edwyn D. James, Morristown, Tennessee

BLONDE BROWNIES

1 c. flour	1 c. brown sugar
1/2 tsp. baking powder	1 egg, beaten
1/8 tsp. salt	1 tsp. vanilla
1/8 tsp. soda	1 6-oz. package chocolate chips
1/2 c. chopped nuts	
1/3 c. butter	

Sift the dry ingredients together and add the nuts. Melt the butter and mix in the brown sugar, egg and vanilla. Add the flour mixture to the butter mixture and mix. Spread in a square baking pan. Sprinkle chocolate chips over the top. Bake for 25 minutes at 350 degrees. Cut into squares.

Mrs. Paul W. Frazier, Grenada, Mississippi

CHEWY SQUARES

1 stick butter	2 c. self-rising flour
1 box light brown sugar	1 tsp. vanilla
2 eggs	1 c. chopped nuts

Melt the butter in top of a double boiler, then add the sugar. Remove from heat and add the eggs, one at a time, beating well after each addition. Do not use electric mixer. Add flour, vanilla and nuts and mix well. Pour in a greased 13 x 9 x 2-inch pan. Bake at 350 degrees for 20 minutes. Cool and cut into squares.

Mrs. F. H. Rimer, Blythewood, South Carolina

WALNUT TREASURE SQUARES

1/2 c. shortening
1 c. (packed) brown sugar
1 egg
1/4 c. milk
1/4 c. sherry
1 2/3 c. sifted all-purpose
    flour
1 tbsp. instant coffee powder
3/4 tsp. salt

1/2 tsp. baking powder
1/2 tsp. soda
1/2 tsp. cinnamon
1 c. coarsely chopped California
    walnuts
1 c. semisweet chocolate
    morsels
Icing

Cream the shortening, sugar and egg in a bowl, then stir in the milk and sherry. Batter may look curdled but will smooth out when flour is added. Sift the flour with coffee powder, salt, baking powder, soda and cinnamon. Add to the creamed mixture and blend until smooth. Stir in the walnuts and chocolate morsels and spread in a greased 10 x 15-inch baking pan. Bake at 375 degrees for about 20 minutes or until top springs back when lightly touched. Cool in the pan. Spread with Icing and decorate with additional walnuts and chocolate morsels. Cut into squares. About 36 squares.

Icing

2 1/4 c. sifted powdered
    sugar
1 1/2 tbsp. soft butter

2 tbsp. sherry
1 tbsp. milk
1 tsp. instant coffee powder

Combine all ingredients in a bowl and beat until smooth.

DESSERT HEROES

2 pkg. brownie mix with nuts
Angostura aromatic bitters

1/2 gal. brick-type vanilla
ice cream

Prepare the brownie mix according to package directions, adding 3 tablespoons angostura aromatic bitters with the water. Place in 2 well-greased 9-inch square pans. Bake according to package directions, then cool. Cut each panful into nine 3-inch squares. Cut the ice cream into 3-inch squares and place on 9 brownie squares. Sprinkle with several drops of angostura aromatic bitters and top with remaining brownies. Wrap in plastic wrap and store in freezer until ready to serve.

COCONUT-PECAN SQUARES

1/2 c. butter
1/2 c. dark brown sugar
Flour
2 eggs
1 c. light brown sugar

1 c. coarsely chopped pecans
1/2 c. shredded coconut
1 tsp. vanilla
Pinch of salt
Powdered sugar

Cream the butter and dark brown sugar together and add 1 cup flour, then mix well. Press mixture into a greased 8 x 8 x 2-inch pan, spreading evenly into corners. Bake at 350 degrees for 20 minutes. Beat eggs until frothy, add light brown sugar gradually and beat until thick. Toss the pecans and coconut with 2 tablespoons flour and mix into egg mixture. Stir in vanilla and salt and mix well. Spread over baked mixture. Bake for 20 minutes longer or until well browned. Cool, then sprinkle with powdered sugar and cut into 1-inch squares. 2 dozen.

Mrs. Naomi Smith, Greensboro, North Carolina

LEMON-COCONUT SQUARES

Flour
1/2 c. butter
1 1/2 c. brown sugar
2 eggs, beaten
1 1/2 c. flaked coconut
1 c. chopped nuts

1/2 tsp. baking powder
1/4 tsp. salt
1/2 tsp. vanilla
1 c. powdered sugar
1 tbsp. melted butter
Juice of 1 lemon

Combine 1 1/2 cups flour, butter and 1/2 cup brown sugar and mix well. Pat into a buttered 9 x 13-inch pan. Bake at 275 degrees for 10 minutes. Combine eggs and remaining brown sugar and mix well. Combine 2 tablespoons flour with the coconut, nuts, baking powder and salt. Mix into the egg mixture, then stir in the vanilla. Spread over the baked mixture. Bake at 350 degrees for 20 minutes. Combine the remaining ingredients and spread over the top. Cut into squares.

Mrs. Joe Hurst, Newport, Tennessee

LEMON-NUT SQUARES

1 lb. butter or margarine
2 c. sugar
6 eggs
3 1/2 c. flour
1 tsp. baking powder

Pinch of salt
4 c. chopped pecans
1 15-oz. box raisins, floured
1 2-oz. bottle lemon extract

Cream the butter and sugar in a large bowl and add the eggs, one at a time, beating well after each addition. Sift the dry ingredients together and add to egg mixture. Fold in the remaining ingredients. Pour into 2 greased and floured loaf pans. Bake for 2 hours and 30 minutes at 250 degrees. Refrigerate for several hours. Cut into thick slices, then cut slices into squares. These squares may be frosted.

Mrs. H. M. McKay, Baytown, Texas

LEMON SOURS

3/4 c. sifted flour
1/3 c. butter or margarine
2 eggs
1 c. (packed) brown sugar
3/4 c. shredded coconut
1/2 c. chopped nuts

1/8 tsp. baking powder
1/2 tsp. vanilla
1 tsp. grated lemon rind
1 1/2 tbsp. lemon juice
2/3 c. (about) confectioners'
    sugar

Mix the flour and butter together until crumbly, then sprinkle in an 11 x 7-inch pan. Bake for 10 minutes in a 350-degree oven. Beat the eggs and mix in the brown sugar, coconut, nuts, baking powder and vanilla. Spread on the baked mixture, then return to the oven and bake for 20 minutes longer. Mix the lemon rind and juice with the confectioners' sugar to make a creamy icing and spread over the top. Cool and cut into squares.

Mrs. A. Richard Stirni, Alexandria, Virginia

NOUGAT

4 c. ground pecans	6 egg whites, stiffly beaten
2 c. sugar	1/2 stick butter, melted

Mix the pecans and sugar and fold into the egg whites. Add the melted butter and mix well. Spread in a well-greased pan. Bake at 250 to 300 degrees until brown. Cut into squares.

Ruby F. Ducrest, St. Martinville, Louisiana

PARTY SQUARES

1 c. sifted flour	3 egg whites
1 tsp. baking powder	1 tsp. vanilla
1/4 tsp. salt	1 1/2 c. chopped nuts
1 1/2 c. light brown sugar	

Sift the flour, baking powder and salt together, then mix with the sugar. Add the egg whites and mix well, then stir in vanilla and nuts. Pour into a greased and floured 8 x 8-inch pan. Bake at 350 degrees for 25 to 30 minutes. Cool for 5 minutes and cut into squares.

Mrs. J. A. Mayes, Llano, Texas

PEANUT-MERINGUE SQUARES

2 c. all-purpose flour	3/4 c. salad oil
1/2 tsp. salt	Vanilla to taste
1 tsp. baking powder	1/2 c. roasted peanuts
1/2 tsp. soda	1/2 c. grated chocolate
2 eggs, separated	1/2 c. sugar
1 c. (firmly packed) brown sugar	

Mix the flour, salt, baking powder and soda. Beat the egg yolks in a bowl until thick and stir in the brown sugar, oil and vanilla. Stir in dry ingredients and spread in 2 greased 8-inch square pans. Sprinkle peanuts and chocolate over top. Beat the egg whites in a bowl until stiff. Add sugar gradually, beating constantly, and spread over chocolate mixture. Bake at 325 degrees for 40 minutes. Cool and cut into 2-inch squares.

Mrs. George Pecsek, Virginia Beach, Virginia

PEANUT SQUARES

3/4 c. butter or margarine	2 c. all-purpose flour
1 c. (firmly packed) brown sugar	1/4 tsp. salt
1 egg, separated	2 tsp. cinnamon
1 tsp. vanilla	3/4 c. chopped peanuts

Cream the butter and sugar in a bowl. Add the egg yolk and vanilla and mix thoroughly. Sift dry ingredients together. Add to butter mixture and blend well. Press into greased cookie pan. Beat the egg yolk slightly and spread over flour mixture. Sprinkle peanuts over top and mark in squares with dull knife. Bake in 325-degree oven for 30 minutes or until done. Crease squares again with knife and cool before removing from pan.

Mrs. Walter T. Davis, Macon, Georgia

TWIN BAKE-IN-BULK COOKIES

1 c. fine dry bread crumbs	1 3/4 c. sifted flour
1 1/2 c. sugar	1/2 tsp. salt
1 tsp. cinnamon	1 6-oz. package semisweet
1/2 c. melted butter or	chocolate morsels
margarine	1 c. chopped California walnuts
1 c. butter or margarine	1 6-oz. package butterscotch
2 eggs	morsels
1 tsp. almond extract	

Combine the bread crumbs, 3/4 cup sugar and cinnamon. Add the melted butter and mix well. Press half the mixture into 2 greased 8 x 8 x 2-inch pans or a 9 x 13 x 2-inch pan. Cream the butter and remaining sugar in a bowl, then beat in eggs, one at a time. Add the almond extract and beat until light and fluffy. Sift the flour and salt together and stir into creamed mixture. Divide mixture in half. Add chocolate morsels and 1/2 cup walnuts to half the mixture and add butterscotch morsels and remaining walnuts to other half. Spoon chocolate mixture over crumbs in 1 baking pan, spreading gently to cover. Spoon butterscotch mixture over crumbs in remaining pan and spread gently. Spread chocolate mixture over 1/2 of the crumbs and butterscotch mixture over other half if 1 pan is used. Sprinkle tops with remaining crumb mixture and press lightly. Bake at 350 degrees for 35 to 40 minutes. Cool and cut in 1 1/4-inch squares. About 6 dozen.

shaped
& rolled
cookies

At Christmas time . . . for children's parties . . . on almost any special occasion, creative homemakers turn to shaped and rolled cookies for delectable treats.

For an old-fashioned Christmas tree, decorate with holiday cookies. After cutting rolled cookies into appropriate shapes, press both ends of a six-inch string into the top of the cookie. Or make a hole in the cookie top with the eraser end of a pencil and, after the cookies are baked, thread string through the opening. For a new taste treat this holiday season, try making Chocolate Christmas Sugar Cookies – their unusual blend of flavors makes them unforgettable.

To highlight a child's birthday party, decorate a frosted cake with circus cutouts – clowns, seals balancing balls, even brightly colored stars. Prepare these cutouts from a rolled cookie recipe, and even they will be edible!

In this section, you'll not only find just-right sugar cookie recipes but recipes for shaped cookies as well. Cookie Jar Gingersnaps will fill your jar – and satisfy your family's craving for something sweet between meals. Peanut Butter Cookies – one of America's favorites – are a welcome addition to school lunch boxes. And these are just some of the recipes awaiting you in the pages that follow, pages you're sure to turn to again and again for really special shaped and rolled cookies.

43

PETER PANIC BUTTONS

1 c. crunchy peanut butter	1 egg
1/2 c. butter	1 1/2 c. sifted flour
1/2 c. sugar	3/4 tsp. soda
1/2 c. (firmly-packed) brown	1/2 tsp. baking powder
sugar	1/4 tsp. salt
1/2 tsp. vanilla	5 doz. candy-coated chocolates

Cream the peanut butter and butter in a bowl. Add sugars gradually and cream until light and fluffy. Add the vanilla and egg and beat well. Sift the flour with soda, baking powder and salt. Add to creamed mixture and mix thoroughly. Chill dough if necessary. Shape into balls, using a heaping teaspoon for each, and place on cookie sheet. Bake in 375-degree oven for 10 to 12 minutes or until golden brown. Top each cookie with a candy-coated chocolate and cool on racks. 5 dozen.

ALMOND TEA COOKIES

1 1/2 c. margarine	1 c. chopped almonds
1 c. sugar	4 tbsp. instant tea
2 egg yolks	2 tbsp. milk
1 tsp. almond extract	2 1/2 c. sifted powdered sugar
2 c. sifted flour	Almond halves

Cream 1 cup margarine in a bowl. Add sugar and beat until light and fluffy. Add the egg yolks and almond extract and blend well. Add flour and chopped almonds and mix thoroughly. Shape into 1-inch balls and place on ungreased baking sheet. Press balls to 1/4-inch thickness. Bake at 325 degrees for 15 minutes. Remove from baking sheet and cool. Dissolve the tea in milk. Cream remaining margarine in a bowl until light and fluffy. Add powdered sugar and tea mixture and beat until smooth. Frost cookies and top with almond halves. 4 dozen.

Mrs. B. E. Hallister, Tulsa, Oklahoma

BACHELOR BUTTONS

1 c. butter	2 c. flour
1 c. (packed) light brown sugar	1 tsp. soda
1 egg	1 c. chopped nuts
1/8 tsp. salt	1 c. flaked coconut

Cream the butter and sugar in a bowl. Add the egg and mix well. Add remaining ingredients and mix. Roll into 1-inch balls and place on greased cookie sheet. Press centers in with finger. Bake at 400 degrees for 10 minutes. 5 dozen.

Mrs. Robert L. Dayberry, Lawndale, North Carolina

BUTTER BALLS

2 sticks butter	2 c. flour
3/4 c. sifted powdered sugar	2 tbsp. water
1 tsp. vanilla	1 c. ground pecans

Cream the butter in a bowl. Add the sugar gradually and beat until light. Add vanilla and mix. Add the flour alternately with water and stir in the pecans. Shape into balls and place on ungreased cookie sheet. Bake at 350 degrees for 12 to 15 minutes. Sprinkle with additional powdered sugar.

Mrs. Emily E. Jervey, Decatur, Georgia

DATE-CHERRY WINKS

2 1/4 c. flour	2 tbsp. milk
1 tsp. baking powder	1 tsp. vanilla
1/2 tsp. soda	1 c. chopped pecans
1/2 tsp. salt	1 c. chopped dates
3/4 c. shortening	1/3 c. chopped cherries
1 c. sugar	2 1/2 c. crushed corn flakes
2 eggs	Cherry halves

Sift first 4 ingredients together. Cream shortening and sugar well in a bowl. Add the eggs, milk and vanilla and mix. Blend in dry ingredients and mix well. Add pecans, dates and chopped cherries and mix well. Shape into balls, using 1 teaspoon for each, and roll in corn flakes. Place on a greased cookie sheet and top each cookie with a cherry half. Bake for 10 to 12 minutes at 375 degrees. 5 dozen.

Diana Behnke, Little Rock, Arkansas

PECAN CURLS

1/2 c. sifted flour	1 tsp. vanilla
1/4 tsp. soda	3/4 c. finely chopped pecans
1 c. (firmly-packed) brown sugar	3/4 c. quick or old-fashioned
3/4 c. soft butter or margarine	rolled oats
2 eggs	2 tbsp. confectioners' sugar

Preheat oven to 350 degrees. Sift flour and soda together into a bowl. Add the brown sugar, butter, eggs and vanilla and beat for about 2 minutes or until smooth. Blend in pecans and oats and drop by teaspoonfuls onto well-greased cookie sheet about 3 inches apart. Bake for 8 to 10 minutes or until brown around edges. Cool for about 1 minute, then remove from cookie sheet carefully with a wide spatula. Turn upside down over rolling pin or several straight-sided glasses wrapped in paper towels or napkins. Cool completely before removing from rolling pin. Sift confectioners' sugar into a small, flat bowl and dip edge of each cookie into sugar carefully. 4 dozen.

CHOCOLATE SNOWCAPS

1 1/4 c. sifted all-purpose	2 c. sugar
flour	4 eggs
2 tsp. baking powder	1 tsp. vanilla
1 tsp. salt	3/4 c. chopped nuts
4 1-oz. squares unsweetened	1 c. whole bran cereal
chocolate	1/2 c. sifted confectioners'
1/4 c. soft shortening	sugar

Sift the flour, baking powder and salt together. Melt the chocolate and shortening in top of a double boiler over hot, not boiling, water. Remove from heat, pour into a mixing bowl and cool. Add the sugar and mix well. Add the eggs, one at a time, beating well after each addition, then stir in vanilla. Add sifted ingredients, nuts and cereal and mix well. Chill for 45 minutes or until stiff enough to form into balls. Shape into balls, using 1 tablespoon dough for each, and roll in confectioners' sugar. Place on greased baking sheets. Bake in 350-degree oven for about 15 minutes or until done. Cool slightly and remove from baking sheets. Cool on wire racks. Cookies will be soft when done but will harden while cooling. 5 dozen.

Photograph for this recipe on cover.

COOKIE JAR GINGERSNAPS

2 c. sifted flour	3/4 c. shortening
1 tbsp. ginger	1 c. sugar
2 tsp. soda	1 egg
1 tsp. cinnamon	1/4 c. molasses
1/2 tsp. salt	

Sift the flour, ginger, soda, cinnamon and salt together twice. Cream the shortening in a bowl and add sugar gradually, beating after each addition until blended. Beat in the egg and molasses. Add flour mixture and blend well. Shape into balls, using 1 teaspoon dough for each, and roll in additional sugar to coat. Place 2 inches apart on ungreased cookie sheet. Bake in 350-degree oven for 12 to 15 minutes or until lightly browned and cracked.

Mrs. L. C. Lake, Mineral Wells, Texas

CREAM CHEESE COOKIES

1 c. sifted flour	1 3-oz. package cream cheese
2 tsp. baking powder	1 tsp. vanilla
1/8 tsp. salt	1/4 tsp. almond flavoring
1/2 c. sugar	Crushed whole wheat flakes
1/2 c. butter	Coarsely crushed pecans

Sift the flour, baking powder and salt together. Cream the sugar, butter, cream cheese and flavorings in a bowl and stir in flour mixture. Chill. Shape into walnut-sized balls and roll in wheat flakes. Place on ungreased cookie sheet 2 inches apart and top each cookie with pecans. Bake at 350 degrees for 15 minutes and cool on rack. 3 dozen.

Mrs. Ralph Penix, Piney Flats, Tennessee

CIRCUS COOKIES

3/4 c. butter	4 egg yolks
1 c. sugar	2 c. sifted flour
1 tsp. vanilla	Walnut halves

Cream the butter and sugar in a bowl and stir in the vanilla and egg yolks. Add the flour and mix well. Chill for 30 minutes. Roll in small balls and place on greased cookie sheet. Press a walnut half into each cookie. Bake for 10 to 12 minutes at 375 degrees. 4 dozen.

Mrs. James Quigley, Orange, Texas

CHERRY WINKS

4 c. corn flakes
2 1/4 c. sifted all-purpose
   flour
1 tsp. baking powder
1/2 tsp. soda
1/2 tsp. salt
3/4 c. softened margarine or
   butter
1 c. sugar

2 eggs
2 tbsp. milk
1 tsp. vanilla
1 c. chopped nuts
1 c. finely chopped dates
1/3 c. finely chopped
   maraschino cherries
18 maraschino cherries, cut in
   quarters

Crush the corn flakes into coarse crumbs. Sift the flour, baking powder, soda and salt together. Place the margarine and sugar in a mixing bowl and beat until light and fluffy. Add the eggs and beat well. Stir in the milk and vanilla. Add the sifted ingredients, nuts, dates and chopped cherries and mix well. Shape into balls, using 1 tablespoon dough for each, and roll in crushed corn flakes. Place on greased baking sheets and top each cookie with a cherry quarter. Bake in 375-degree oven for about 12 minutes or until lightly browned. Remove from baking sheets immediately and cool on wire racks. Three cups oven-toasted rice cereal may be substituted for corn flakes. 5 1/2 dozen.

Photograph for this recipe on cover.

GUMDROP COOKIES

1/2 c. shortening
1/2 c. sugar
1/2 c. brown sugar
1 egg
1/2 tsp. vanilla
1/2 tsp. soda
1 1/2 tsp. cold water

1 1/4 c. flour
1/2 tsp. baking powder
1/2 tsp. salt
1 c. rolled oats
1/2 c. shredded coconut
3/4 c. chopped gumdrops
Powdered sugar

Cream the shortening, sugar and brown sugar in a bowl and stir in the egg and vanilla. Dissolve soda in cold water and stir into creamed mixture. Sift flour, baking powder and salt together and blend with creamed mixture. Stir in the oats, coconut and gumdrops. Shape into balls the size of a walnut and place 1 inch apart on greased baking sheet. Bake at 375 degrees for 12 minutes. Remove from oven and sprinkle with powdered sugar. Cool slightly before removing from baking sheet.

Janice Y. Skinner, Tuscaloosa, Alabama

BUTTER CRISPS

1 c. butter
1   3-oz. package cream cheese
1 c. sugar
1 egg yolk
1 tsp. vanilla

2 1/4 c. sifted all-purpose
   flour
1/2 tsp. salt
1/4 tsp. baking powder

Preheat oven to 350 degrees. Cream the butter and cream cheese in a mixing bowl. Add the sugar gradually and beat until light and fluffy. Beat in egg yolk and vanilla. Sift the flour, salt and baking powder together and add to creamed mixture gradually. Pack into cookie press and press onto ungreased baking sheet. Bake for 12 to 15 minutes. Remove to wire rack to cool. Dough may be tinted different colors before baking and sprinkled with colored sugar or cinnamon sugar. Cookies may be decorated with a tinted frosting after baking. 8 dozen.

COFFEE BONBONS

1 c. butter	1 tbsp. instant coffee
3/4 c. confectioners' sugar	Chocolate Confectioners'
1/2 tsp. vanilla	Frosting
1 3/4 c. sifted all-purpose	1/3 c. chopped nuts (opt.)
flour	

Preheat oven to 350 degrees. Cream the butter in a mixing bowl. Add sugar gradually and beat until light and fluffy. Blend in vanilla. Sift the flour and coffee together and add to creamed mixture gradually. Chill for several hours for ease in handling. Shape into balls 1 inch in diameter and place on baking sheets. Bake for 15 to 20 minutes. Dip balls while warm in additional confectioners' sugar and place on wire rack to cool. May be cooled completely on wire rack, and frosted with Chocolate Confectioners' Frosting. Sprinkle with nuts. 4 dozen.

Chocolate Confectioners' Frosting

1 3/4 c. confectioners' sugar	2 tbsp. butter, softened
1 1/2 tbsp. cocoa	2 tbsp. milk

Mix the sugar, cocoa, butter and milk in a small bowl until smooth.

DECORATED BUTTERSCOTCH COOKIES

1 6-oz. package butterscotch morsels	1/2 tsp. salt
1 3-oz. package cream cheese, at room temperature	1 1/2 c. sifted all-purpose flour
1/4 c. sugar	1/2 c. semisweet chocolate morsels
1 egg yolk	1 tbsp. shortening
1/4 tsp. almond extract	

Melt the butterscotch morsels in top of a double boiler over hot, not boiling, water, then remove from water. Blend in the cream cheese. Stir in the sugar and beat in the egg yolk. Add almond extract and salt, then blend in flour gradually. Pack into a cookie press and press in desired shapes onto ungreased baking sheet. Bake in 350-degree oven for 10 to 13 minutes. Remove at once from baking sheet and cool on rack. Melt the chocolate morsels and shortening in top of double boiler over hot, not boiling, water and spoon on cookies. Decorate with nuts, dragees, cinnamon candies, tinted coconut and glaceed fruit. 3-4 dozen.

Photograph for this recipe on page 1.

NUTMEG COOKIE LOGS

3 c. flour	2 tsp. vanilla
1 tsp. nutmeg	2 tsp. rum flavoring
1 c. butter	Frosting
3/4 c. sugar	Nutmeg
1 egg	

Sift flour and nutmeg together. Cream the butter in a bowl. Add sugar gradually and cream well. Blend in egg and flavorings. Add flour mixture and mix well. Shape pieces of dough into long rolls 1/2 inch in diameter and cut in 3-inch lengths. Place on ungreased cookie sheet. Bake at 350 degrees for 12 to 15 minutes or until golden brown, then cool. Spread Frosting on cookies and score Frosting with tines of fork to resemble bark. Sprinkle with nutmeg.

Frosting

3 tbsp. butter	1 c. powdered sugar
1/2 tsp. vanilla	Evaporated milk
1 tsp. rum flavoring	

Cream first 4 ingredients in a bowl. Add enough evaporated milk, if needed, to thin frosting.

Betty Kandt, Herington, Kansas

NUT CAKES

1 c. margarine	1 c. finely chopped nuts
3/4 c. sugar	2 c. flour
1 c. fine bread crumbs	1 egg

Mix all ingredients in a bowl. Shape or roll into finger-sized pieces and flatten with fork lengthwise. Place on a greased baking sheet. Bake at 350 degrees for about 15 minutes. 5 1/2 dozen.

COCONUT TOPS

6 tbsp. evaporated milk	1 egg, beaten
3 c. flaked coconut	Flour
5/8 c. sugar	

Mix the milk, coconut, sugar and egg in a bowl. Shape into small balls and place on a greased baking sheet sprinkled with flour. Bake at 375 degrees for 12 to 15 minutes or until golden brown. 2 1/2 dozen.

WAFER-THIN OAT CAKES

1 1/4 c. oats	5/8 c. melted margarine
3/4 c. sugar	1/4 c. milk
1/4 c. light molasses or	1 c. flour
golden syrup	1/2 tsp. baking powder

Mix all ingredients in a bowl. Drop from teaspoon about 3 inches apart onto a greased baking sheet. Bake at 350 degrees for about 8 minutes or until light brown. Let stand for 1 minute, then remove from baking sheet with a spatula. Shape around a rolling pin or large glass and cool. 5 dozen.

GRANDMA HOWSER'S GINGER COOKIES

3/4 c. shortening	2 tsp. ginger
2 1/2 c. sugar	1 tsp. nutmeg
2 eggs, well beaten	1 tsp. cloves
1 1/2 c. dark molasses	1 tsp. allspice
Grated rind of 1 lemon	2 tsp. soda
Grated rind of 1 orange	8 c. (about) flour
4 tsp. cinnamon	

Cream the shortening and sugar in a bowl and stir in eggs, then molasses and grated rinds. Mix the spices and soda with half the flour and stir into creamed mixture. Add enough remaining flour to make medium-stiff dough and chill. Roll out very thin on a floured surface and cut with cookie cutter. Place on a greased cookie sheet. Bake in 350-degree oven for 8 to 10 minutes. Store in tightly covered container. 28 dozen.

Mrs. William Howser, Lanham, Maryland

MACADAMIA-SUGAR BALL COOKIES

1 c. soft butter	1/4 tsp. salt
Powdered sugar	3/4 c. finely chopped
1 tsp. vanilla	macadamia nuts
2 1/2 c. sifted flour	Powdered sugar

Cream the butter and 1/2 cup powdered sugar in a bowl until blended. Add vanilla. Sift the flour with salt and stir into creamed mixture. Add nuts and blend well. Shape into 1-inch balls and place on an ungreased cookie sheet. Bake at 400 degrees for about 10 minutes or until set but not browned. Place on rack with waxed paper under rack and sift powdered sugar over cookies. 6 dozen.

Mrs. Eve Burwell, Ebenezer, Mississippi

PEANUT BUTTER COOKIES

1 2/3 c. sifted flour	1 c. peanut butter
1 1/2 tsp. baking powder	1/3 c. light corn syrup
Dash of salt	1 egg, beaten
1/2 c. margarine	1/2 tsp. vanilla
1/2 c. brown sugar	

Sift the flour, baking powder and salt together. Cream the margarine in a bowl. Add sugar gradually and cream until light and fluffy. Add 1/2 cup peanut butter and syrup and beat until smooth and blended. Add the egg and vanilla. Add the sifted ingredients, a small amount at a time, mixing well after each addition. Shape dough into 1-inch balls and place on ungreased cookie sheet. Flatten with a fork. Place remaining peanut butter on cookies, placing 1/2 teaspoon on top of each. Bake in 350-degree oven for 12 to 15 minutes. 3 1/2 dozen.

Mrs. Perry Brock, Chandler, North Carolina

SAND COOKIES

1 c. butter	3 c. flour
4 tbsp. powdered sugar	1 c. chopped pecans

Cream the butter and powdered sugar in a bowl. Add flour and pecans gradually and mix well. Shape into small rolls about 1 1/2 inches long and place on an ungreased cookie sheet. Bake at 325 degrees for 20 minutes or until golden brown. Roll in additional powdered sugar while hot. 5 dozen.

Mrs. Mary B. Hodson, Lockport, Louisiana

HOLIDAY COOKIES

3 c. sifted flour	1/2 tsp. cloves
1 c. (firmly packed) brown sugar	1/2 tsp. nutmeg
1/2 tsp. baking powder	1 c. margarine
1 1/2 tsp. cinnamon	2 eggs, slightly beaten
1/2 to 1 tsp. ginger	1 tsp. vanilla
	Decorator's Frosting

Sift the flour, sugar, baking powder and spices into a mixing bowl and cut in the margarine until mixture resembles fine crumbs. Stir in the eggs and vanilla until smooth. Chill. Roll out dough, 1/3 at a time, to 1/8-inch thickness on a floured board. Cut into 5-inch rounds, using a coffee can lid or a large cutter, and place on an ungreased cookie sheet. Bake in 375-degree oven for 10 to 12 minutes or until edges are very lightly browned. Frost with Decorator's Frosting.

Decorator's Frosting

1 c. softened margarine	Food colorings
1 lb. sifted confectioners' sugar	

Combine the margarine and sugar in a bowl and beat until smooth. Divide into several parts and tint with desired food colorings. Chill for 30 minutes. Spread on cookies and decorate with frosting, using decorating tube. Blend in several drops of water if frosting becomes too stiff.

BUTTER COOKIES

1 3/4 c. flour	1 egg, well beaten
1/2 tsp. baking powder	1/2 tsp. vanilla
2/3 c. softened butter	1 sq. chocolate, melted (opt.)
1/2 c. sugar	

Sift the flour and baking powder together. Cream the butter and sugar in a bowl and mix in the egg. Add vanilla. Stir in sifted ingredients gradually and mix until smooth. Cool the chocolate and stir into half the dough. Roll out each mixture 1/8 inch thick on a floured board and cut into desired shapes. Place on ungreased cookie sheet. Bake at 400 degrees for 6 to 8 minutes or until brown. 3 dozen.

Mrs. Charles Byrd, Marion, North Carolina

FROSTED RAISIN TOASTIES

1 c. California seedless raisins	2 1/2 c. sifted flour
2 c. rolled oats	1 tsp. soda
1 c. broken walnuts	1/2 tsp. salt
1 c. mixed shortening and butter	1 tsp. cinnamon
or margarine	1/2 c. milk
2 c. (packed) brown sugar	2 c. powdered sugar
3 eggs, beaten	

Chop raisins lightly. Place the oats and walnuts on a baking sheet. Bake at 400 degrees for about 8 minutes or until lightly toasted. Cream the shortening mixture and sugar well in a bowl and beat in eggs. Sift flour, soda, salt and cinnamon together and add to creamed mixture alternately with milk. Stir in the raisins, oats and walnuts. Divide into 6 parts and chill. Roll out each part on a floured surface to 15 x 1-inch strip and place, 2 strips at a time, on a lightly greased baking sheet. Press to 4-inch strip with rolling pin. Bake at 375 degrees for 12 to 15 minutes. Combine the powdered sugar with 2 tablespoons hot water and brush on warm strips. Sprinkle with additional raisins and turn raisins to coat with frosting. Cool. Cut each strip into 12 diagonal slices. 6 dozen.

Photograph for this recipe on page 42.

CHOCOLATE CHRISTMAS SUGAR COOKIES

3/4 c. shortening	1/4 c. light corn syrup
1 c. sugar	2 c. flour
1 egg	1/4 tsp. salt
2 sq. unsweetened chocolate,	1 tsp. soda
melted	1 tsp. cinnamon

Cream the shortening, sugar and egg in a bowl and stir in the chocolate and corn syrup. Sift dry ingredients together and stir into creamed mixture. Chill for 1 hour. Roll out 1/8 inch thick on well-floured pastry cloth and cut into desired shapes. Place on ungreased cookie sheet. Bake at 350 degrees for 10 to 12 minutes. Frost and decorate, if desired. 2 1/2 dozen.

Martha Kay Johnston, Quitman, Arkansas

DATE COOKIES

1 1/2 c. sugar	1 tsp. vanilla
1 c. shortening	3 1/2 c. flour
2 eggs, beaten	1 tsp. baking powder
2 tbsp. cream	1 c. chopped dates

Cream the sugar and shortening in a bowl and stir in the eggs, cream and vanilla. Sift flour and baking powder together and stir into creamed mixture. Stir in the dates. Roll out thin on a floured surface and cut in desired shapes. Place on a greased cookie sheet. Bake for 8 to 10 minutes at 350 degrees. 4 dozen.

Mrs. Viola Y. Grubbs, Mt. Sterling, Kentucky

OATMEAL-BUTTER COOKIES

1 c. butter or margarine	2 c. sifted all-purpose flour
3/4 c. (firmly packed) light brown sugar	3/4 c. quick or old-fashioned oats

Preheat oven to 300 degrees. Cream the butter in a bowl. Add sugar gradually and beat until fluffy. Add the flour and blend well. Stir in the oats. Roll out on a lightly floured board or canvas to 1/8-inch thickness and cut into bells, circles or flowers with floured cookie cutters. Place on lightly greased cookie sheets. Bake for 20 to 25 minutes, then cool. Sprinkle with confectioners' sugar, if desired. About 4 dozen.

DECORATOR'S COOKIES

1/2 c. shortening	1 tbsp. almond extract
1 c. sugar	3 1/2 c. flour
2 eggs	2 tsp. baking powder
2 tbsp. milk	

Cream the shortening and sugar in a bowl until light and fluffy. Add the eggs, milk and almond extract and beat well. Sift dry ingredients together and stir into creamed mixture. Cover and chill thoroughly. Roll out 1/4 inch thick on a floured board and cut with cookie cutter. Place on lightly greased baking sheet. Bake at 375 degrees for about 8 minutes. Cool and cut in desired shapes.

Decorator's Frosting

1 c. shortening	1 tsp. almond extract
1/4 c. milk	Food colorings
1 1-lb. box powdered sugar	

Beat the shortening in a bowl with electric mixer at high speed until creamy. Add remaining ingredients except food colorings and beat for about 10 minutes. Divide and place in small bowls. Tint with desired food colorings and spread on cookies.

Mrs. Pittman L. Wingo, Birmingham, Alabama

OLD-TIME SUGAR COOKIES

2 c. flour	2/3 c. shortening
3/4 tsp. baking powder	2 eggs
1/4 tsp. salt	3/4 tsp. vanilla
3/4 c. sugar	

Sift dry ingredients together into a bowl and cut in shortening. Add the eggs and vanilla and mix well. Roll out very thin on floured board and cut with floured cookie cutter. Place on a greased cookie sheet. Bake at 400 degrees for 9 to 12 minutes. 4 dozen.

Mrs. Neal Cullar, Bonham, Texas

THIN COOKIES

1 c. butter	1 tbsp. milk
1 c. sugar	2 tsp. baking powder
1 egg	Flour

Cream the butter and sugar in a bowl. Add egg and milk and mix well. Add the baking powder and enough flour to make thick dough and mix well. Roll out very thin on a floured surface and cut with cookie cutter. Place on a greased cookie sheet. Bake at 325 degrees until brown. 4 dozen.

Mrs. Doc Savell, Philadelphia, Mississippi

PEPPERMINT ROUNDS

1 c. softened butter or
  margarine
1/2 c. sugar
1 egg
1 tsp. vanilla
2 1/2 c. sifted all-purpose
  flour
1/2 tsp. salt

1 c. rolled oats
1/3 c. crushed peppermint
  candy
Confectioners' sugar
White confectioners' sugar
  frosting
Thin red confectioners' sugar
  frosting

Preheat oven to 350 degrees. Cream the butter in a bowl and add sugar gradually. Blend in the egg and vanilla. Sift flour and salt together and add to creamed mixture gradually. Stir in oats and peppermint candy and chill thoroughly. Roll out to 1/8-inch thickness on board or canvas lightly dusted with confectioners' sugar and cut with floured 2 1/2-inch round cutter. Place on greased cookie sheets. Bake for 8 to 10 minutes, then cool. Frost with white confectioners' sugar frosting. Make several lines across each frosted cookie with red confectioners' sugar frosting before white frosting sets. Draw a toothpick lightly back and forth across the lines to give a pretty swirled look. 4 dozen.

CHOCOLATE DECORATING DIP

1 12-oz. package semisweet
  chocolate morsels

2 c. sifted confectioners' sugar
1 sm. can evaporated milk

Prepare favorite recipe for rolled cookies or use prepared cookie mix, following package directions for rolled cookies. Cut into desired shapes and bake. Cool. Melt the chocolate morsels over hot, not boiling, water. Add the confectioners' sugar and evaporated milk and beat until smooth. Keep over hot water so mixture will not thicken. Dip cookies, place on waxed paper and let stand until set. 2 cups.

Photograph for this recipe on page 5.

drop cookies

Drop cookies may be called the hardiest members of the cookie family. Recipes for these cookies usually yield several dozen – enough to fill the biggest, emptiest cookie jar. What's more, drop cookies travel well, making them favorites in college dorms, overseas bases, and anywhere thoughtful mothers mail these sweets.

Southern mothers know that drop cookies are also easy to prepare – most recipes can be mixed in just one bowl and in only a few minutes. As a result, they have developed many kinds of drop cookies to satisfy the hungry appetites of growing families. Now the best of these recipes are shared with you in the section which follows.

Birthday Frosted Jewels or Spice Cookie Lollypops might be just what you need to greet a birthday child when he comes home from school – how nice to remember his special day even with his milk-and-cookies snack. Sugarless Carrot Cookies were developed especially for the eater who has to eliminate certain foods from his diet – but doesn't want to shut out flavor as well. Even traditional southern foods are used to prepare cookies, as in recipes for Pecan Clusters and Fruitcake Cookies.

To fill a cookie jar ... to remember someone with his favorite sweet snack ... or on any occasion when you want to serve cookies, turn to this section. You're certain to find just the drop cookies recipe you want!

BASIC COOKIES

1 c. (packed) brown sugar	2 1/2 c. flour
1 c. sugar	1 tsp. salt
1 c. soft shortening	1 tsp. soda
2 eggs	

Cream the sugars, shortening and eggs in a bowl. Mix the flour, salt and soda. Add to creamed mixture and mix well. Drop onto a greased cookie sheet. Bake at 350 degrees for 15 to 18 minutes. 6-7 dozen.

Mrs. David V. De Hart, Anderson, South Carolina

BANANA-DATE CIRCLES

3/4 c. soft butter	1 c. mashed bananas
1 c. sugar	1 1/2 c. quick oats
1 egg	1 c. chopped dates
1 1/4 c. flour	1/2 c. chopped nuts
3/4 tsp. salt	1 6-oz. package butterscotch
1/2 tsp. baking powder	pieces
1/2 tsp. nutmeg	

Cream the butter and sugar in a bowl and stir in the egg. Sift dry ingredients and stir into creamed mixture. Add remaining ingredients and mix well. Drop from spoon onto greased cookie sheet. Bake at 400 degrees for 10 to 12 minutes. 6 dozen.

Mabel Brown, Miami, Florida

BANANA SPICE COOKIES

1/2 c. soft shortening	1/4 tsp. soda
1 c. brown sugar	1/4 tsp. salt
2 eggs	1/4 tsp. cloves
1 c. mashed bananas	1/2 tsp. cinnamon
2 c. sifted flour	1/2 c. chopped nuts
2 tsp. baking powder	Thin powdered sugar icing

Preheat oven to 325 degrees. Mix the shortening, sugar and eggs in a bowl and stir in bananas. Sift dry ingredients together and stir into sugar mixture. Blend in nuts and chill for 1 hour. Drop by tablespoonfuls 2 inches apart on lightly greased baking sheet. Bake for 8 to 10 minutes. Cool and frost with powdered sugar icing. 2 1/2 dozen.

Gene Johnson, Brownfield, Texas

BIRTHDAY FROSTED JEWELS

1/2 c. shortening	1/2 c. sugar
1 1/2 c. chopped raisins	1 egg

1/2 c. molasses	2 tsp. allspice
2 1/2 c. flour	1 tsp. soda
1 tsp. salt	1 c. water or milk

Mix the shortening, raisins and sugar in a bowl and blend in egg and molasses. Combine the flour, salt and allspice. Dissolve the soda in water. Add dry ingredients to raisin mixture alternately with water mixture and drop by teaspoonfuls onto greased baking sheet. Bake at 375 degrees for 8 minutes, then cool.

Brown Butter Icing

3 tbsp. butter	2 1/2 tbsp. water
1 1/2 c. powdered sugar	

Heat the butter in a saucepan until light brown. Stir in the sugar and water and beat until smooth. Frost cookies.

S. M. Knox, Miami, Florida

PINEAPPLE-RAISIN COOKIES

1 c. (firmly packed) golden brown sugar	3/4 c. undrained crushed pineapple
1/2 c. soft butter or margarine	2 c. sifted all-purpose flour
1 egg	1 tsp. baking powder
1 tsp. vanilla	1/2 tsp. soda
1/2 c. raisins	1/2 tsp. salt
	1/2 c. chopped walnuts

Place the sugar, butter, egg and vanilla in a bowl and beat until fluffy. Add the raisins and pineapple. Sift the flour with baking powder, soda and salt. Add the pineapple mixture and mix well. Stir in the walnuts. Drop by spoonfuls 2 inches apart on greased cookie sheet. Bake in 375-degree oven for 12 to 15 minutes or until lightly browned. 4 dozen.

CHOCOLATE FRUIT JEWELS

1 c. sifted all-purpose flour
2 tsp. cinnamon
1 tsp. baking powder
1/2 tsp. salt
1/2 tsp. nutmeg
1/4 tsp. cloves
1/2 c. (firmly packed) brown
  sugar
1/4 c. butter or margarine

1/2 c. evaporated milk
1 6-oz. package semisweet
  chocolate morsels
1 c. coarsely chopped
  California walnuts
2 c. chopped mixed candied
  fruit
1 c. raisins
1 tbsp. grated orange rind

Sift the flour, cinnamon, baking powder, salt, nutmeg and cloves together. Combine the brown sugar and butter in a bowl and beat until creamy. Stir in the flour mixture alternately with evaporated milk. Add the chocolate morsels, walnuts, candied fruit, raisins and orange rind and blend well. Drop by heaping teaspoonfuls on greased cookie sheets. Bake in a 375-degree oven for 12 to 14 minutes, then cool. Base of cookies may be glazed by dipping in Chocolate Decorating Dip, if desired. About 7 dozen.

Photograph for this recipe on page 5.

TOLL HOUSE COOKIES

1 c. softened butter or
  margarine
3/4 c. sugar
3/4 c. (firmly packed) brown
  sugar
1 tsp. vanilla
1/2 tsp. water
2 eggs

2 1/4 c. sifted all-purpose
  flour
1 tsp. soda
1 tsp. salt
1 c. chopped California
  walnuts
1 12-oz. package chocolate
  morsels

Cream the butter, sugars, vanilla and water in a bowl, then beat in the eggs. Sift flour, soda and salt together and stir into butter mixture. Add the walnuts and chocolate morsels and mix well. Drop by well-rounded half teaspoonfuls on greased baking sheet. Bake in a 375-degree oven for 10 to 12 minutes. Cool. About 8 dozen.

Photograph for this recipe on page 5.

BROWN SUGAR COOKIES

1 egg white
1 c. (packed) light brown sugar
1/8 tsp. salt

1 tbsp. flour
1 c. chopped nuts

Beat egg white until stiff. Add sugar gradually, beating constantly. Fold in remaining ingredients and drop by teaspoonfuls onto greased cookie sheet. Bake at 300 degrees for about 15 minutes.

Mrs. C. M. Brennan, Montgomery, Alabama

BUCKAROONS

2 c. sifted flour	2 eggs
1 tsp. soda	2 c. rolled oats
1/2 tsp. salt	1 tsp. vanilla
1/2 tsp. baking powder	1 6-oz. package chocolate
1 c. shortening	pieces
1 c. sugar	1 c. chopped nuts (opt.)
1 c. (packed) brown sugar	Milk

Sift flour, soda, salt and baking powder together. Blend the shortening and sugars in a bowl. Add eggs and beat until light and fluffy. Add flour mixture and mix well. Add oats, vanilla, chocolate pieces and nuts and mix. Add small amount of milk to hold ingredients together, if needed. Drop by teaspoonfuls onto greased cookie sheet. Bake for 15 minutes in 350-degree oven. 11 dozen.

Mrs. Jean Sutherland, College Station, Texas

LACE COOKIES

1/2 c. butter or margarine	1/4 tsp. salt
1/2 c. sugar	1 c. quick-cooking oats
1/3 c. sifted all-purpose	2 tbsp. milk
flour	

Preheat oven to 375 degrees. Melt the butter in a saucepan. Stir in remaining ingredients and mix well. Drop by half teaspoonfuls about 3 inches apart onto greased and floured cookie sheets and spread thin with a spatula. Bake for 5 to 7 minutes or until edges are brown. Remove from oven and let stand for 1 minute. Remove from cookie sheets carefully with a wide spatula. Cookies will be very thin and lacy. Cool thoroughly. 3 1/2 dozen.

OAT COOKIES

1 1/4 c. rolled oats	5/8 c. margarine
1 5/8 c. flour	6 tbsp. milk
1/2 tsp. salt	Butter
1/2 tsp. baking powder	Marmalade

Mix all ingredients except butter and marmalade in a bowl. Drop by spoonfuls onto a greased baking sheet and flatten with a glass dipped in flour. Bake at 400 degrees for about 5 minutes. Serve with butter and marmalade.

ALMOND-CARROT COOKIES

1 c. shortening	2 1/2 c. flour
3/4 c. sugar	2 tsp. baking powder
1 egg	1 tsp. salt
1 c. ground carrots	1 c. powdered sugar
1/2 tsp. vanilla	1 tbsp. orange juice
1/2 tsp. almond flavoring	

Cream the shortening and sugar in a bowl. Add egg and mix well. Add the carrots and flavorings and mix well. Sift the flour, baking powder and salt together and stir into the carrot mixture. Drop from teaspoon on greased baking sheet. Bake at 350 degrees until light brown, then cool. Mix the powdered sugar and orange juice and spread on cookies. 4-5 dozen.

Mrs. Fred Thaxter, Wilmington, North Carolina

SUPERB WALNUT COOKIES

1/2 c. shortening	2 eggs, well beaten
1/2 tsp. salt	3/4 c. flour, sifted
1 tsp. vanilla	3/4 c. chopped walnuts
1 c. sugar	

Cream the shortening, salt and vanilla in a bowl. Add the sugar gradually and cream well. Add the eggs and mix thoroughly. Add the flour and walnuts and mix well. Drop from a teaspoon onto greased baking sheets and flatten with a glass dipped in flour. Bake at 325 degrees for 12 to 15 minutes. 30 cookies.

Photograph for this recipe on page 58.

SUGARLESS CARROT COOKIES

1/2 c. shortening	1/2 tsp. salt
2 tbsp. liquid sweetener	1 c. sieved cooked carrots
1 egg, beaten	1 tsp. vanilla
1 1/2 c. flour	1/2 c. chopped nuts
2 tsp. baking powder	1/2 c. raisins (opt.)

Cream the shortening, sweetener and egg in a bowl. Sift the dry ingredients together and add to the creamed mixture alternately with carrots. Stir in the vanilla, nuts and raisins and drop by teaspoonfuls onto lightly greased cookie sheet. Bake at 350 degrees until lightly browned. Do not overbake.

Mrs. W. S. Gordon, Malvern, Arkansas

FRESH APPLE COOKIES

1/2 c. shortening	1 egg
1/2 tsp. salt	1/2 c. sour milk
1 1/2 c. (packed) brown sugar	1 c. seedless raisins
1 tsp. nutmeg	1 c. unpeeled chopped apples
1 tsp. cinnamon	2 c. flour
1/2 tsp. cloves	1/2 c. chopped nuts
1 tsp. soda	

Mix all ingredients in a bowl in order listed. Drop by teaspoonfuls onto baking sheet. Bake at 400 degrees for 11 to 14 minutes. Cool slightly.

Icing

1 1/2 c. powdered sugar	Pinch of salt
1/2 tsp. vanilla	Cream

Mix the sugar, vanilla and salt in a bowl and add enough cream for spreading consistency. Spread on warm cookies.

Mrs. Verner G. Smith, Prosperity, South Carolina

COCONUT-CORN FLAKE DROPS

1 c. shortening	1 tsp. baking powder
1 c. (packed) brown sugar	1 tsp. soda
1 c. sugar	2 c. oats
2 eggs	2 c. corn flakes
2 c. flour	1 c. shredded coconut
1/2 tsp. salt	1 tsp. vanilla

Mix the shortening and sugars in a bowl. Add eggs and mix well. Sift the flour with salt, baking powder and soda and mix with sugar mixture until well blended. Add the oats and corn flakes and mix. Add the coconut and vanilla and blend thoroughly. Drop by teaspoonfuls on greased cookie sheet. Bake at 350 degrees for 15 minutes. 4 dozen.

Mrs. Clara Mae Fields, Kingsport, Tennessee

COCONUT DROP COOKIES

1 c. butter	1 tsp. soda
1 c. (packed) brown sugar	1 1/2 tsp. salt
1 c. sugar	1 c. oats
2 eggs	2 c. flaked coconut
2 1/2 c. flour	1 tsp. vanilla
1 1/2 tsp. baking powder	

Cream the butter and sugars in a bowl. Add the eggs, one at a time, beating well after each addition. Sift the flour, baking powder, soda and salt together and stir into the creamed mixture. Add remaining ingredients and mix well. Drop from teaspoon on ungreased baking sheet. Bake at 350 degrees until lightly browned.

Mrs. Robert L. Moore, Huntsville, Alabama

FRUITCAKE COOKIES

3 sticks margarine	4 eggs
1 1/4 c. sugar	2 tbsp. wine
3 c. flour	1 lb. diced candied cherries
1/2 tsp. cloves	1 lb. diced candied pineapple
1/2 tsp. cinnamon	2 qt. chopped pecans
1/2 tsp. allspice	

Cream the margarine and sugar in a bowl. Add flour and spices and mix well. Add the eggs, one at a time, beating well after each addition. Add the wine, fruits and pecans and mix well. Drop by teaspoonfuls on greased cookie sheet. Bake for 15 minutes at 350 degrees, having pan of water on bottom rack of oven.

Mrs. R. M. Rowell, Elba, Alabama

GINGER DROP COOKIES

1/2 c. lard or butter	2 1/2 c. flour
1/2 c. (packed) brown sugar	1 tsp. soda
1/4 c. sugar	1 1/2 tsp. ginger
1 egg	1/2 tsp. cinnamon
1/2 c. molasses	1/2 tsp. nutmeg
1/4 c. sour milk	

Cream the lard and sugars in a bowl. Add the egg and beat well. Mix the molasses and sour milk. Mix dry ingredients together and add to creamed mixture alternately with molasses mixture. Drop by teaspoonfuls onto greased and floured baking sheet. Bake at 450 degrees until brown.

Mrs. Dixie Scott, Crockett, Virginia

HERMITS

3 1/2 c. flour, sifted	1/2 c. shredded coconut
2 c. (packed) brown sugar	1 c. peanuts
1/2 tsp. baking powder	2 eggs
1/2 tsp. salt	3/4 c. salad oil
1 tsp. soda	1/2 c. cold coffee
1 c. seedless raisins	

Mix the flour with sugar, baking powder, salt and soda into a bowl and mix in raisins, coconut and peanuts. Beat the eggs and stir in oil and coffee. Add all at once to flour mixture and stir until well blended. Drop by spoonfuls onto a well-greased baking sheet. Bake at 375 degrees for 12 to 15 minutes. 6 1/2 dozen.

Mrs. George Pecsek, Virginia Beach, Virginia

HOLIDAY GEMS

1 c. (firmly packed) brown sugar	1 1/2 lb. chopped pecans
1 stick butter	1/2 tsp. soda
4 eggs	1/4 tsp. salt
3 c. flour	1 tsp. nutmeg (opt.)
1 lb. chopped candied cherries	3 tbsp. buttermilk
1 lb. chopped candied pineapple	1/2 c. cooking sherry
1 lb. white raisins	

Cream the sugar and butter in a bowl until fluffy. Add the eggs, one at a time, beating well after each addition. Mix 1 cup flour with fruits and pecans. Sift the remaining flour with soda, salt and nutmeg. Stir the buttermilk into creamed mixture, then add soda mixture alternately with sherry. Add fruit mixture and mix well. Drop by teaspoonfuls onto ungreased cookie sheet. Bake at 375 degrees for 15 minutes or until brown.

Mrs. Otto Murphy, Springfield, Tennessee

TWO-TONE WALNUT JUMBLES

1/4 c. soft shortening	2 3/4 c. sifted all-purpose
1/4 c. butter	flour
1 c. (packed) brown sugar	1/2 tsp. soda
1/2 c. sugar	1 tsp. salt
1 tsp. vanilla	1 c. sour cream
2 eggs	1 1-oz. square unsweetened
1 1/2 c. chopped California	chocolate, melted
walnuts	

Cream the shortening, butter, sugars and vanilla well in a bowl. Add the eggs and beat until fluffy. Stir in 1 cup walnuts. Sift the flour with soda and salt and add to creamed mixture alternately with sour cream. Drop half the dough in small mounds, 2 inches apart, on greased cookie sheets. Stir melted chocolate into remaining dough and drop a mound of equal size touching each of the plain mounds. Mounds will bake together as 1 cookie. Sprinkle with remaining walnuts. Bake at 375 degrees for about 15 minutes until lightly browned. Remove to wire racks to cool thoroughly before storing. 18 to 24 jumbles.

DROP SUGAR COOKIES

2 1/2 c. flour	3/4 tsp. salt
1/2 tsp. soda	1 c. butter

1 c. sugar
1 tsp. vanilla
1 egg, beaten

2 tbsp. milk
1/2 c. chopped nuts
Colored sugar

Have all ingredients at room temperature. Sift first 3 ingredients together. Cream the butter, sugar and vanilla in a bowl. Add the egg and beat until mixed. Stir in flour mixture, then the milk and nuts. Drop from teaspoon onto greased cookie sheet and flatten with bottom of water glass dipped in colored sugar. Bake for 12 minutes at 400 degrees. 5-6 dozen.

Velma Lee, Littleton, North Carolina

LEMON-ICED COOKIES

1 c. shortening
2 c. sugar
2 eggs
3 1/2 c. flour
1 tsp. soda
1 tsp. baking powder

1 c. buttermilk
Juice and grated rind of
 1 orange
2 c. powdered sugar
Juice and grated rind of
 2 lemons

Cream the shortening and sugar in a bowl and stir in the eggs. Sift dry ingredients together and add to creamed mixture alternately with buttermilk. Add orange juice and rind and mix. Drop from teaspoon onto greased cookie sheet. Bake at 400 degrees for 12 minutes. Mix remaining ingredients in a bowl with electric mixer at high speed until thick and smooth. Spread on warm cookies.

Mrs. Henry Burson, Columbia, South Carolina

ORANGE COOKIES

3/4 c. shortening
1 1/2 c. (packed) brown sugar
2 eggs
1 1/2 tsp. grated orange rind
1 tsp. vanilla
1/2 c. sour milk

1/2 tsp. soda
3 c. flour
1 1/2 tsp. baking powder
Pinch of salt
1/2 c. chopped nuts

Cream the shortening and sugar in a bowl. Add the eggs, grated rind and vanilla and mix well. Mix the sour milk and soda. Sift dry ingredients together and add to creamed mixture alternately with milk mixture. Stir in the nuts and drop by spoonfuls onto greased baking sheet.Bake at 400 degrees until done.

Glaze

1 1/2 tsp. grated orange rind
1/3 c. orange juice

1 c. sugar

Combine all ingredients in a bowl. Cover each cookie with 1 1/2 tablespoons of the Glaze.

Mrs. Cleo Matthews, Davenport, Oklahoma

MINCEMEAT DROP COOKIES

3/4 c. shortening	3/4 tsp. salt
1 1/2 c. sugar	1 9-oz. package mincemeat
3 eggs, well beaten	3 tbsp. water
3 c. sifted flour	1 c. broken walnuts
1 tsp. soda	

Cream the shortening and sugar thoroughly in a bowl. Add eggs and beat well. Sift dry ingredients together and add half the dry ingredients to creamed mixture. Crumble the mincemeat and add to the egg mixture. Add the water and stir until blended. Add walnuts and remaining flour mixture and mix well. Drop from teaspoon onto greased cookie sheet. Bake in 350-degree oven for 10 to 15 minutes. One cup canned mincemeat may be substituted for packaged mincemeat. Omit water. 4 dozen.

Mrs. Esther Iaquinto, Morgantown, West Virginia

OATMEAL LOAFERS

1 c. flour	1/4 c. milk
1/2 c. sugar	1/2 c. salad oil
2 tsp. baking powder	1 tsp. vanilla
1/4 tsp. salt	1 egg, beaten
1 1/2 c. quick oats	Whole peanuts
1 c. chopped peanuts	

Sift the flour, sugar, baking powder and salt in a bowl. Mix remaining ingredients except whole peanuts. Add all at once to the flour mixture and mix well. Drop by spoonfuls onto greased cookie sheet and decorate tops with whole peanuts. Bake at 375 degrees for about 15 minutes. 3 dozen.

Mrs. George Pecsek, Virginia Beach, Virginia

SOFT PEANUT BUTTER COOKIES

2/3 c. shortening	2 eggs
1/2 c. peanut butter	2 c. sifted flour
2/3 c. (firmly packed) light brown sugar	2 tsp. baking powder
2/3 c. sugar	1/2 c. evaporated milk
1 tsp. vanilla	1 c. chopped peanuts

Cream the shortening and peanut butter in a bowl and stir in sugars and vanilla. Add the eggs, one at a time, beating well after each addition. Sift dry ingredients together and add to creamed mixture alternately with undiluted milk. Add the peanuts and mix well. Drop by teaspoonfuls onto greased cookie sheet. Bake at 350 degrees for about 12 minutes. 5 dozen.

Mrs. F. John Mann, Clearwater, Florida

PEANUT-OATMEAL COOKIES

2 c. self-rising flour	1/2 c. seedless raisins
2 c. quick-cooking oats	2 eggs
1 c. sugar	1 c. melted margarine
1 c. (packed) brown sugar	1/4 tsp. soda
1 c. parched peanuts	4 tbsp. hot water
1 c. flaked coconut	

Mix the flour, oats, sugars, peanuts, coconut and raisins in a bowl. Add eggs and margarine and mix well. Dissolve the soda in water and stir into the oats mixture. Drop by spoonfuls onto greased cookie sheet. Bake at 400 degrees for 8 to 10 minutes. 4 dozen.

Mrs. J. F. Kersey, Tampa, Florida

RAISIN MUNCHING COOKIES

1/2 c. butter	1/2 tsp. salt
1 c. (packed) brown sugar	1/2 c. toasted wheat germ
1 egg	2/3 c. California seedless
1 tsp. vanilla	raisins
1 c. sifted flour	1/2 c. butterscotch chips
1/2 tsp. baking powder	

Blend the butter, sugar, egg and vanilla in a bowl. Sift the flour with baking powder and salt. Add to the butter mixture and mix well. Stir in wheat germ, raisins and butterscotch chips and drop by teaspoonfuls onto lightly greased baking sheet about 2 inches apart. Bake at 375 degrees for 10 to 12 minutes or until browned. Cool slightly, then remove to racks to cool. About 3 1/2 dozen.

SPICE COOKIE LOLLIPOPS

1/2 c. butter or margarine	1/2 tsp. cloves
1/2 c. sugar	1/2 tsp. nutmeg
1 egg	1/4 c. lukewarm water
1/2 c. molasses	Confectioners' sugar
2 1/2 c. sifted flour	Red or green food coloring
1/4 tsp. salt	1 6-oz. package semisweet
1 tsp. soda	chocolate bits
1 tsp. ginger	24 tiny red gumdrops
1/2 tsp. cinnamon	

Preheat oven to 375 degrees. Place the butter and sugar in a medium bowl and beat with mixer at medium speed until light and fluffy. Add egg and beat well. Beat in molasses. Sift the flour, salt, soda, ginger, cinnamon, cloves and nutmeg together and add to creamed mixture alternately with water, beating at low speed after each addition until smooth. Drop from heaping tablespoon onto ungreased cookie sheet about 4 inches apart and insert a wooden skewer in each with a twisting motion. Bake for about 10 minutes. Cool slightly and remove to wire rack to cool. Mix desired amount of confectioners' sugar with just enough water to moisten and tint pink or green. Spread on cookies. Decorate with chocolate bits for eyes, tips of gumdrops for noses and remaining gumdrops for mouths. 2 dozen.

Mrs. Andrew J. Taylor, Little Rock, Arkansas

◁ WALNUT ROCKY ROAD DROPS

1/2 c. butter	1/2 tsp. soda
2/3 c. (packed) brown sugar	3/4 tsp. salt
1 tsp. vanilla	1 tsp. instant coffee powder
1 egg, beaten	1/3 c. milk
1/2 c. semisweet chocolate morsels, melted	12 to 14 marshmallows
	36 to 40 California walnut halves and/or lge. pieces
1/2 c. chopped California walnuts	Chocolate Frosting
1 1/2 c. sifted all-purpose flour	

Cream the butter, sugar and vanilla in a bowl until light and fluffy, then beat in the egg. Add the melted chocolate and chopped walnuts and mix well. Sift the flour with soda, salt and coffee powder. Add to creamed mixture alternately with milk and stir until well blended. Drop by rounded teaspoonfuls onto greased cookie sheets. Bake at 350 degrees for 10 minutes or just until cookies are done. Do not overbake. Cut the marshmallows crosswise into thirds. Top each cookie with a marshmallow slice and bake for 1 minute longer to set marshmallows. Remove cookies to wire racks and top each marshmallow with a walnut half, pressing down lightly. Cool. Place racks over waxed paper and carefully ladle warm Chocolate Frosting over top of each. Let stand until set. Frosting on waxed paper may be scraped up and reheated to use again. 3-3 1/4 dozen.

Chocolate Frosting

1/4 c. butter or margarine	1/4 tsp. salt
1/3 c. milk or light cream	1 tsp. vanilla
1/2 c. semisweet chocolate morsels	2 1/2 c. sifted powdered sugar

Combine the butter, milk and chocolate in top of double boiler. Place over hot, not boiling, water until melted and smooth, stirring occasionally. Add salt and vanilla and beat in powdered sugar until smooth. Double Frosting recipe if a double-thick frosting is desired. Heavy coating will make an almost candy-like cookie.

PECAN CLUSTERS

1/4 c. butter or margarine	Vanilla to taste
1/2 c. sugar	1/2 c. sifted flour
1 egg	1/4 tsp. baking powder
1 1/2 sq. unsweetened chocolate, melted	1/2 tsp. salt
	2 c. broken pecans

Cream the butter and sugar in a bowl. Add egg, chocolate and vanilla and mix well. Sift flour, baking powder and salt together and stir into creamed mixture. Add the pecans and mix. Drop from teaspoon onto greased baking sheet. Bake at 350 degrees for 10 minutes. 1 1/2 dozen.

Jessie B. Lynch, Corsicana, Texas

foreign cookies

Many of our favorite cookie recipes are borrowings — traditional recipes of other nations brought to America by immigrants and incorporated into our recipe files. Even the word "cookie" comes from the Dutch *koekje,* which means tiny cake.

Southern homemakers have long borrowed recipes from their neighbors. Many of these recipes had their origins in other lands. So it was that English Savoy Cookies or French Napoleons may have been brought to the Southland by its earliest settlers. From Germany has come a recipe for German Lebkuchen, a flaky and mildly flavored cookie which captures so well the German love for pastry-like treats. From Italy have come Italian Roses, delicate and elaborate cookies which date back to the early pastry chefs of the Medici court. Mexico, lying against the region's southernmost border, shares its recipe for Mexican Wedding Cakes — a very special cookie served only on important occasions.

These are just some of the recipes awaiting you in the section which follows. All have been adapted to American tastes and cooking methods by skilled southern women who wanted to share the best of foreign cookies with their families and friends. Now they share these prized recipes with you in the hope that you will enjoy them as much as they have!

75

CHINESE BARS

3/4 c. soft butter	1 c. chopped nuts
Flour	1 c. shredded coconut
3 tbsp. brown sugar	1 c. powdered sugar
2 eggs, beaten	Juice of 1 lemon
1 tsp. baking powder	Cream
1 c. chopped dates	

Mix the butter, 1 1/2 cups flour and brown sugar in a bowl, then press into a greased 10-inch square pan. Bake at 300 degrees for 10 minutes. Beat the eggs in a bowl. Add the baking powder and 2 tablespoons flour and mix. Stir in the dates, nuts and coconut and spread over baked mixture. Bake for 25 minutes longer. Combine the powdered sugar and lemon juice in a bowl and add enough cream for spreading consistency. Spread over hot date mixture and cool. Cut into squares.

Mrs. Vickie Salter, Meridian, Mississippi

CHINESE ALMOND CAKES

2 1/2 c. flour	1 tbsp. orange juice
1 tsp. baking powder	2 tsp. almond extract
1/4 tsp. salt	1 tsp. vanilla
1 egg	1 egg, slightly beaten
3/4 c. sugar	1 tbsp. water
2/3 c. corn oil	1/3 c. blanched almonds

Mix the flour, baking powder and salt. Beat the egg thoroughly in a mixing bowl and add sugar gradually, beating well. Mix the corn oil, orange juice, almond extract and vanilla and add to egg mixture gradually, beating until well mixed. Beat in 1/2 of the flour mixture, then fold in remaining flour mixture. Knead lightly on a floured surface until smooth. Form into 1-inch balls and place on greased baking sheet. Flatten with fingers or fork. Combine the beaten egg and water and brush lightly on tops of cookies. Place almond on center of each. Bake in 350-degree oven for about 12 minutes or until lightly browned. About 3 dozen.

Photograph for this recipe on page 74.

CZECHOSLOVAKIAN BAR COOKIES

2 sticks margarine	2 c. flour
1 c. sugar	1 c. chopped pecans
2 egg yolks	1/2 c. strawberry jam

Cream the margarine and sugar in a bowl. Add egg yolks, flour and pecans and mix thoroughly. Spread half the mixture in an 8-inch square pan. Mash the strawberry jam and spread over pecan mixture. Spread remaining pecan mixture over jam. Bake at 375 degrees until brown. Cut in squares. 2 dozen.

Mrs. Lucy B. Taylor, Warren, Arkansas

DANISH CARDAMOM COOKIES

1 3/4 c. butter	2 tsp. baking powder
2 c. sugar	1 tbsp. powdered cardamom seed
1 sm. egg	1 1/4 c. cream
8 c. flour	2 c. finely chopped almonds

Cream the butter and sugar in a bowl and stir in the egg. Sift dry ingredients together and add to creamed mixture alternately with cream. Stir in the almonds. Knead on a floured surface until smooth. Shape into a roll and wrap in waxed paper. Refrigerate overnight. Slice about 1/4 inch thick and place on a greased cookie sheet. Bake at 350 degrees for 10 to 15 minutes.

Mrs. Elaine McKee, Anacoco, Louisiana

DANISH BLUEBERRY STRIPS

2 pkg. dry yeast	1/2 tsp. ground cardamom
1/4 c. lukewarm water	4 c. all-purpose flour
1 c. lukewarm milk	2 c. fresh blueberries
1/2 c. soft butter	1/2 c. confectioners' sugar
2 eggs, well beaten	1/2 c. chopped pecans
1/4 c. sugar	Confectioners' sugar glaze
1/4 tsp. nutmeg	

Sprinkle the yeast into lukewarm water in a bowl. Let stand for 5 minutes, then stir to blend. Add the milk and mix. Add the butter, eggs, sugar and spices and mix well. Add flour and beat until dough pulls off the mixing spoon. Let rise until doubled in bulk. Turn out on a heavily floured board and knead until smooth and elastic. Roll out into a 16 x 18-inch rectangle and cut into halves. Place half the dough on a greased cookie sheet. Rinse and drain the blueberries, then mix with confectioners' sugar and pecans. Spread over the dough and place remaining dough over the filling. Press together to push out all air and seal edges. Let rise until doubled in bulk. Bake at 375 degrees for 25 to 30 minutes or until browned, then cool on a rack. Cut into 1 x 5-inch strips with a sharp knife and decorate strips with confectioners' sugar glaze.

DUTCH SANTA CLAUS COOKIES

2 c. butter	1/2 tsp. cloves
2 c. sugar	1/4 tsp. salt
4 c. sifted flour	1/2 tsp. soda
4 tsp. cinnamon	1/2 c. sour cream
1/2 tsp. nutmeg	1/2 c. chopped nuts

Cream the butter with sugar in a bowl. Sift flour with spices, salt and soda and add to creamed mixture alternately with sour cream. Add the nuts and knead well on a floured surface. Shape into a roll and wrap in waxed paper. Refrigerate overnight. Slice and place on a cookie sheet. Bake at 400 degrees until browned.

Betty Jane Powell, Nathalie, Virginia

DUTCH FRUIT SQUARES

1/2 lb. butter	1 c. sour cream
3 c. flour	Grated rind of 1 lemon
1 c. sugar	1 tsp. lemon juice
1 tsp. baking powder	1 sm. jar raspberry preserves
1 tsp. soda	Chopped nuts to taste
4 egg yolks	Powdered sugar
1/2 tsp. salt	

Mix the butter and flour in a bowl as for pie crust. Add remaining ingredients except preserves, nuts and powdered sugar and mix well. Spread in ungreased 11 x 16-inch cookie pan. Spread preserves on top and sprinkle with nuts. Bake at 325 degrees for 30 minutes. Sprinkle with powdered sugar and cut into squares.

Mrs. Mary Nemetz, Hopewell, Virginia

ENGLISH SAVOY COOKIES

3 eggs, separated	1 1/4 c. self-rising flour
3/4 c. confectioners' sugar	1 c. cornmeal

Beat the egg whites in a bowl until stiff but not dry. Fold in the sugar gradually, then fold in the beaten egg yolks. Sift the flour and cornmeal together and fold into the egg mixture gradually. Place in a pastry bag with 1/2-inch tip and pipe into 3 1/2-inch lengths on brown paper-lined baking sheet. Sprinkle with additional sugar and shake off excess sugar. Bake at 425 degrees for about 5 minutes, then cool. Dampen the brown paper and remove cookies.

Mrs. Maryanne Turner, Dallas, Texas

FRENCH NAPOLEONS

1 1/8 c. butter	1 tsp. vanilla
1/4 c. sugar	1 egg, slightly beaten
1/4 c. cocoa	2 c. graham cracker crumbs

1 c. flaked coconut
3 tbsp. milk
1 3 3/4-oz. package instant
   vanilla pudding mix

2 c. sifted confectioners' sugar
1 6-oz. package chocolate
   chips
1 tbsp. paraffin (opt.)

Combine 1/2 cup butter, sugar, cocoa and vanilla in top of a double boiler and cook over hot water until butter melts. Stir in the egg quickly and cook, stirring, for about 3 minutes or until thick. Stir in the crumbs and coconut and press into a greased 9-inch square pan. Cream 1/2 cup butter in a bowl. Stir in the milk, pudding mix and confectioners' sugar and beat until light and fluffy. Spread over coconut mixture and chill until firm. Place the chocolate, remaining butter and paraffin in a heatproof bowl and melt over hot water. Cool, then spread over pudding mixture. Chill and cut in squares.

Mrs. C. R. Hobson, Knoxville, Tennessee

FRENCH RAISIN COOKIES

3 c. flour
2 c. (packed) brown sugar
1 tsp. soda
1 tsp. baking powder
1/2 tsp. salt
1 c. hot water

2 eggs, beaten
1 c. melted shortening
1 tsp. vanilla
1 c. raisins
1/2 c. chopped nuts
Butter frosting

Sift the flour, brown sugar, soda, baking powder and salt together into a bowl. Add remaining ingredients except butter frosting and stir until well mixed. Place in a greased jelly roll pan. Bake at 375 degrees for 15 minutes. Cool and cut into squares. Frost with butter frosting.

Mrs. L. R. Andersen, Louisville, Kentucky

GERMAN LEBKUCHEN

8 c. sifted cake flour
1/2 tsp. soda
1 1/2 tsp. cinnamon
1/4 tsp. cloves
1/4 tsp. nutmeg
1/3 c. strained honey
1 c. (firmly packed) brown
   sugar
1/4 c. water

2 eggs, slightly beaten
1 1/2 c. chopped candied
   orange peel
1 1/2 c. chopped citron
2 c. blanched slivered almonds
2 c. sifted confectioners' sugar
3 tbsp. boiling water
1 tsp. vanilla

Sift the flour with soda and spices 3 times. Mix the honey, brown sugar and water in a saucepan and bring to a boil. Cook for 5 minutes, then cool. Add the flour mixture, eggs, fruits and almonds and mix. Place in a bowl and cover. Refrigerate for 2 to 3 days. Roll out 1/4 inch thick on lightly floured board and cut into 1 x 3-inch strips. Place on greased baking sheet. Bake at 350 degrees for 15 minutes. Cool. Combine the confectioners' sugar and boiling water in a bowl. Add vanilla and beat thoroughly. Spread on cookies. Place in covered container for at least 1 day to ripen.

Mrs. Bernice S. Person, Drewryville, Virginia

GERMAN HUSARENKRAPFEN COOKIES

1 1/4 sticks butter or margarine 1/2 c. sugar 1 egg, separated	1 2/3 c. flour 2 tbsp. grated lemon rind Jelly or nuts

Cream the butter and sugar thoroughly in a bowl. Add the egg yolk and mix well. Blend in the flour and lemon rind and mix thoroughly. Shape into long roll, 1 1/2 inches in diameter. Wrap in waxed paper and chill. Cut in 3/4-inch thick slices and make depression in center of each slice with thumb. Dip top of each cookie in slightly beaten egg white, then in additional sugar. Place jelly in depression and place cookies on ungreased baking sheet. Bake at 350 degrees until medium brown.

Mrs. F. W. Cash, Lincolnton, North Carolina

GERMAN BERLINER KRANTZER WREATHS

3/4 c. butter or margarine 3/4 c. shortening Sugar 2 tbsp. grated orange peel	2 eggs 4 c. sifted flour 1 egg white Green and red colored sugar

Mix the butter, shortening, 1 cup sugar, orange peel and 2 eggs thoroughly in a bowl. Stir in the flour and chill for several hours or overnight. Roll small pieces of dough to diameter of a pencil and 6 inches long and place on an ungreased cookie sheet. Form each to a circle and bring 1 end over and through in a single knot. Beat the egg white until stiff, then beat in 2 tablespoons sugar gradually. Brush tops of cookies with meringue in shape of a bow. Sprinkle wreath with green sugar and bow with red sugar. Bake at 400 degrees for 9 minutes. 4 dozen.

Mrs. Edith Herring, Fort Worth, Texas

GREEK WREATHS

1/2 c. smooth peanut butter 1/3 c. softened butter 2/3 c. sugar 4 eggs 3 c. sifted flour	2 tsp. baking powder 1/4 tsp. salt 1/4 tsp. cinnamon 1/8 tsp. allspice

Cream the peanut butter and butter in a bowl and add sugar gradually. Beat in the eggs, one at a time, then beat until fluffy. Sift remaining ingredients together and stir into creamed mixture gently. Mixture will be soft. Roll 1 tablespoon dough between lightly floured hands to form a 4-inch roll and seal ends together to shape into a wreath. Place on ungreased baking sheet. Bake in 375-degree oven for 8 minutes or until golden brown. Remove to cooling rack immediately.

HUNGARIAN KIFLI COOKIES

1 pkg. yeast	1 egg
6 c. sifted flour	Evaporated milk
1 c. lard	Powdered sugar
1 c. butter	Nut filling
2 egg yolks	

Mix the yeast and flour in a bowl and cut in the lard and butter. Add the egg yolks, egg and enough undiluted milk for stiff dough and mix well. Shape into 3/4-inch balls and place in a bowl. Chill overnight. Roll each ball out on powdered sugar-coated surface and place 1 spoon nut filling on each. Roll as for jelly roll and form in crescent shape. Place on aluminum foil-covered cookie sheet. Bake at 375 degrees for 15 to 20 minutes.

Henrietta Slade, Bessemer, Alabama

HUNGARIAN LOVE LETTERS

3/4 c. butter	3/4 c. powdered sugar
3/4 c. flour	3/4 c. ground walnuts
6 eggs, separated	Cinnamon
Pinch of salt	

Mix the butter and flour in a bowl as for pie crust. Add the beaten egg yolks and salt and mix well. Cover and refrigerate overnight. Beat the egg whites in a bowl until soft peaks form, then beat until stiff, adding sugar gradually. Fold in the walnuts. Divide the chilled pastry into 22 parts and roll each part out on a floured surface to very thin square. Spread walnut mixture in center third of square. Fold 1/3 of the pastry over center third, then fold remaining pastry over. Fold ends over into thirds, forming a square. Place on greased cookie sheet. Bake at 350 degrees for 20 minutes or until golden brown. Remove from cookie sheet at once and cool. Sprinkle with additional sugar and cinnamon.

Mrs. Al Greene, Little Rock, Arkansas

ITALIAN ROSES

12 eggs, beaten	**Flour**
9 tbsp. sugar	**Powdered sugar**

Cream the eggs, sugar and enough flour to make a stiff dough. Roll out thin on a floured surface and cut into strips. Press ends of 3 strips together and braid. Fry in deep, hot fat until lightly browned. Drain and sprinkle with sifted powdered sugar.

Mrs. Charles Tripp, Memphis, Tennessee

ITALIAN CHRISTMAS COOKIES

4 c. sugar	1 tsp. cinnamon
1/2 c. butter	1 tsp. cloves
8 eggs	1/2 c. milk
2 1/2 c. sifted flour	1 tsp. lemon flavoring
Dash of salt	4 c. chopped black walnuts

Cream the sugar and butter in a bowl. Beat in the eggs, one at a time. Sift flour, salt and spices together. Mix the milk and flavoring and add to creamed mixture alternately with flour mixture. Stir in the walnuts and chill. Drop from teaspoon on ungreased baking sheet. Bake in 375-degree oven until lightly browned around edges. Remove from baking sheet immediately.

Mrs. Letha Short, Atlanta, Georgia

ISRAELI PERISHLCAS

1 c. cooked mashed carrots	1 1/4 c. salad oil
Sugar	4 eggs, beaten
2 tsp. cinnamon	2 tsp. vanilla
Juice and grated rind of 1 lemon	1/2 c. warm water
1 c. light seedless raisins	5 c. flour
1/2 c. flaked coconut	2 tsp. baking powder
1 c. ground walnuts	Honey

Combine the carrots, 1/2 cup sugar, cinnamon, lemon juice and rind, raisins, coconut, walnuts and 1/4 cup oil. Mix 1 2/3 cups sugar, eggs, vanilla, remaining oil and water in a bowl. Sift the flour with baking powder and stir into the egg mixture. Roll out on a floured board and cut into small squares. Place 1 teaspoon carrot mixture on each square and fold to make a triangle. Seal edges. Place on a greased baking sheet. Bake at 350 degrees for 25 minutes. Pour small amount of honey over hot cookies immediately and turn to coat all sides.

Mrs. Abe Feinberg, Tallahassee, Florida

LEBANESE SUMBUSIC COOKIES

2 c. melted butter	1 c. sugar
8 c. sifted flour	1/4 tsp. salt

1/2 tsp. dry yeast	Nut filling
1/2 c. warm water	Powdered sugar
1/2 c. warm milk	

Mix the butter, flour, sugar and salt in a bowl and stir in the yeast, water and milk. Let rise for 30 minutes. Roll out, 1 tablespoon at a time, into a circle and place 1 teaspoon nut filling in center. Fold over and seal edge. Form into crescent shapes and prick with fork. Place on baking sheet. Bake at 350 degrees for 20 minutes, then sprinkle with powdered sugar.

Mrs. Sandra Guy, Jacksonville, Florida

MEXICAN SPICY ALMOND WEDGES

2 1/4 c. sifted flour	2/3 c. softened butter or
Salt	margarine
1/2 tsp. baking powder	2 to 3 tbsp. milk
3/4 tsp. cinnamon	1 1/2 c. ground blanched
1/4 tsp. nutmeg	almonds
1/8 tsp. ground cardamom (opt.)	1 1/2 c. sifted powdered sugar
1 1/4 c. (packed) dark brown	1 tsp. almond extract
sugar	1/4 c. orange juice or milk

Sift the flour with 1/2 teaspoon salt, baking powder and spices, then combine with brown sugar in a bowl. Cut in the butter with pastry blender or beat in with electric mixer just until consistency of coarse meal. Stir or beat in milk to make mixture that is consistency of pastry. Press half the mixture into bottom of 2 well-greased 8-inch round pans. Combine the ground almonds, powdered sugar, 1/8 teaspoon salt, almond extract and orange juice and mix well. Spread on flour mixture with a spatula. Crumble remaining flour mixture evenly over top. Bake at 350 degrees for 30 minutes. Cool in pans, invert and cut into wedges. Keep fresh in airtight wrappings. Makes 32 wedges.

MEXICAN WEDDING CAKES

1 c. butter
1/2 c. powdered sugar
2 c. sifted flour

1/4 tsp. salt
1 tsp. vanilla

Cream the butter in a bowl. Add powdered sugar gradually and beat until smooth. Add the flour, salt and vanilla and blend well. Shape into small balls and place on ungreased cookie sheet. Bake at 400 degrees for about 12 minutes and roll in additional powdered sugar.

Pat Dreyer, Oak Ridge, Tennessee

MEXICAN BIZCOCHITOS

2 c. shortening
1 1/2 c. sugar
1 tsp. aniseed
2 eggs, beaten
6 c. sifted flour

3 tsp. baking powder
1 tsp. salt
1/4 c. water
1 tsp. cinnamon

Cream the shortening in a bowl. Add 1 cup sugar and aniseed and mix well. Add the eggs and beat until light and fluffy. Sift the flour, baking powder and salt together and add to creamed mixture. Stir in the water and knead until smooth. Roll out on a floured surface 1/4 inch thick and cut into desired shapes. Mix remaining sugar and cinnamon and sprinkle on cookies. Place cookies on a greased cookie sheet. Bake at 350 degrees until lightly browned.

Ruth M. Bearup, Silver City, New Mexico

MORAVIAN COOKIES

1/2 c. butter or shortening
1 c. molasses
1/3 c. brown sugar
3/4 tsp. ginger
3/4 tsp. cloves
3/4 tsp. cinnamon

1/4 tsp. nutmeg
1/4 tsp. allspice
Dash of salt
3/4 tsp. soda
3 3/4 c. flour, sifted

Place the butter and molasses in a saucepan and heat until butter is melted. Add the sugar, spices, salt and soda and mix well. Add the flour gradually, mixing well after each addition. Cover and refrigerate for about 1 week. Roll out thin on a floured surface and cut with cookie cutter. Place on a baking sheet. Bake at 350 degrees until golden brown.

Mrs. Wade Williard, Winston-Salem, North Carolina

NORWEGIAN SUNDBAKLES

3/4 c. all-vegetable shortening
1/4 c. butter
1 c. sugar

1 egg
3/4 tsp. salt
2 c. sifted flour

Cream the shortening and butter in a bowl until light and fluffy, then add sugar gradually, beating constantly. Beat in the egg and salt. Mix in flour gradually and chill thoroughly. Press about 1 tablespoon dough over bottom and sides of 2 1/4-inch fluted tart pans. Place on baking sheet. Bake in 350-degree oven for 15 minutes or until lightly browned. Cool slightly, then remove from pans, loosening edges with a sharp, pointed knife. Chilled dough may be shaped into 1-inch balls, placed on ungreased baking sheet and topped with candied fruit or nuts before baking, if desired.

NORWEGIAN KRUMKAKER

1 c. butter	1/2 tsp. vanilla
1 c. sugar	2 c. flour
6 eggs	1/2 c. cream, whipped

Cream the butter and sugar in a bowl. Add eggs and vanilla and mix well. Stir in the flour, fold in the whipped cream. Place on timbale iron, 1 tablespoon at a time, and cook in deep, hot fat until brown. Remove from iron and roll in shape of a cone. Serve plain or filled with whipped cream or ice cream. 4 dozen.

Martha Merritt, Raleigh, North Carolina

SCANDINAVIAN FILLED COOKIES

1/2 c. softened butter or margarine	1 c. sifted flour
1/4 c. sugar	1/4 tsp. salt
1 egg, separated	3/4 c. chopped nuts
1/2 tsp. vanilla	Candied fruit or jelly

Cream the butter, sugar, egg yolk and vanilla in a bowl. Sift the flour with salt and stir into creamed mixture. Roll into 1-inch balls. Dip in lightly beaten egg white, then roll in nuts. Place about 1 inch apart on ungreased baking sheet and make indentation in each cookie with thumb. Bake for 20 minutes at 325 degrees, then cool. Place candied fruit in center of each cookie.

Mrs. I. R. Cross, Chattanooga, Tennessee

SWEDISH BUTTER COOKIES

1 c. soft butter	1 1/2 tsp. vanilla
1/2 c. powdered sugar	1 c. finely chopped nuts
2 c. flour, sifted	

Cream the butter and sugar in a bowl. Add flour and vanilla and mix well. Stir in the nuts and chill. Roll into 1/2-inch balls and place on a greased cookie sheet. Bake at 375 degrees for 12 to 15 minutes or until light brown. Roll in additional powdered sugar and store in covered container. 4 dozen.

Mrs. W. T. Smith, Jackson, Mississippi

SWEDISH NUT CRESCENTS

1/4 c. shortening	1 1/3 c. flour
1 1/4 c. sugar	1 tsp. baking powder
1 egg	1/2 tsp. salt
2 tbsp. milk	1 c. chopped pecans
1 tsp. vanilla	

Mix the shortening, 3/4 cup sugar, egg, milk and vanilla in a bowl. Sift the flour, baking powder and salt together and stir into the egg mixture. Spread 1/4 cup dough very thinly and evenly on greased inverted 9 x 9 x 2-inch pan. Mix remaining sugar and pecans and sprinkle small amount on dough. Bake at 325 degrees for 10 to 12 minutes. Cut into 4 1/4 x 3/4-inch strips while hot and shape over rolling pin. Repeat until all dough is used.

Mrs. Alma Little, Mobile, Alabama

SWEDISH SPRITZ COOKIES

1 lb. softened butter	1 tsp. vanilla
1 c. sugar	4 c. sifted flour
1 egg, well beaten	

Preheat oven to 400 degrees. Cream the butter thoroughly in a bowl. Add sugar gradually and beat until light and fluffy. Add the egg and vanilla and beat well. Add flour gradually, beating well after each addition. Force through a cookie press in desired shape onto an ungreased cookie sheet. Bake for 4 to 5 minutes or until brown.

Mrs. D. M. Smith, Grand Prairie, Texas

SWEDISH WEDDING COOKIES

1/4 lb. butter	1 tsp. vanilla
2/3 c. sugar	2 c. oven-toasted rice cereal
1 egg, slightly beaten	3/4 c. chopped walnuts
Pinch of salt	1 c. flaked coconut
1 c. chopped dates	

Combine the butter, sugar, egg, salt and dates in a saucepan and cook for 7 to 10 minutes or until thick. Remove from heat. Add the vanilla, cereal and walnuts and blend well. Form into small balls and roll in coconut. Chill.

Mrs. G. Llewelyn Phillips, Leisure City, Florida

SYRIAN SHORTBREAD COOKIES

1 c. butter
1 c. powdered sugar

2 c. flour

Cream the butter in a bowl and blend in sugar gradually. Stir in flour. Roll out on lightly floured board to 1/4-inch thickness and cut into desired shapes. Place on a cookie sheet. Bake at 300 degrees for 25 minutes or until dry but still white. Cool and remove from cookie sheet.

Mrs. Hugh Beasley, Robbinsville, North Carolina

VIENNESE COCONUT MACAROONS

1/3 c. butter
1/2 c. sugar
2 eggs, well beaten
2 tbsp. heavy cream
1/2 tsp. vanilla

1/2 c. flour
4 tbsp. cornstarch
1/2 tsp. baking powder
1 c. coconut
6 crushed vanilla wafers

Cream the butter and sugar in a bowl. Add the eggs, cream and vanilla and mix well. Sift dry ingredients together and stir into butter mixture. Add the coconut and wafers and mix well. Drop by teaspoonfuls 1 inch apart onto a greased cookie sheet. Bake at 350 degrees for 8 to 10 minutes or until brown. 3 dozen.

Kathryn Woods, Beckley, West Virginia

WELSH TEA COOKIES

2 c. flour
Pinch of cream of tartar
2 tsp. baking powder
3/4 tsp. nutmeg
1/2 tsp. salt

3/4 c. shortening
3/4 c. sugar
1 c. currants
1 egg, beaten
Milk

Sift first 5 ingredients together into a bowl and cut in shortening. Add sugar, currants, egg and enough milk to make a stiff dough and mix well. Refrigerate until chilled. Roll out on a floured surface and cut with cookie cutter. Bake on griddle over medium heat until brown.

Mrs. E. M. Yancey, Annapolis, Maryland

refrigerator & unbaked cookies

When southern homemakers need cookies in a hurry, they naturally turn to refrigerator cookies. And when they don't want to heat up the house by turning on the oven, they depend on unbaked cookies. Together these two make up the "convenience foods" of the cookie family.

Refrigerator cookies are quick and easy to prepare. In fact, why not make a double batch? Use one immediately and save the other for up to two weeks — then bake them on a day when you're in a hurry but want fresh cookies to greet your children coming home from school or friends coming to lunch. This section is packed with recipes designed especially for refrigeration — like Candied Fruit Treats or Date-Nut Rolls.

And on those oh-so-hot days when you can't bear the idea of going near a hot oven, turn to this section for flavorful unbaked cookies every bit as good as their baked counterparts. With recipes like Candied Cookies, Date Balls, or Peanut Butter-Oatmeal Cookies, you'll have your family clamoring for more.

Each recipe in this section is the proud creation of a southern cook, a woman who takes great pride in turning ordinary foods into extraordinary dishes. The result is unforgettable cookies . . . like the refrigerator and unbaked cookie recipes you'll find in this section.

ALMOND STICKS

1 lb. butter	2 c. sugar
4 c. flour	4 eggs, beaten
1 c. water	1 egg white, beaten
1 lb. almond paste	

Blend the butter, flour and water in a bowl and refrigerate overnight. Combine the almond paste, sugar and eggs in a bowl and mix well. Refrigerate overnight. Divide the flour mixture into 8 parts and roll out each part on a floured surface to a circle. Spread almond paste mixture on each circle and roll as for jelly roll. Brush with egg white and place on a greased cookie sheet. Bake for 30 minutes at 350 degrees.

Mrs. Arthur Hall, Muskogee, Oklahoma

BUTTERSCOTCH REFRIGERATOR COOKIES

1 c. soft butter or margarine	3 1/2 c. sifted flour
1 c. (packed) dark brown sugar	1/2 tsp. salt
1 c. sugar	1 tsp. soda
2 eggs	1 c. finely chopped nuts

Combine the butter, sugars and eggs and mix well. Sift the flour, salt and soda together and stir into the butter mixture. Blend in the nuts. Shape dough into 2 rolls and wrap in waxed paper. Chill for several hours or overnight. Slice dough in 1/8-inch thick slices and arrange on ungreased baking sheet. Bake in 400-degree oven for 8 to 10 minutes. 12 dozen cookies.

Mrs. James H. Lamb, Jr., Greene County, Alabama

CANDIED FRUIT TREATS

1 c. butter	2 1/4 c. sifted flour
1 c. powdered sugar	1 c. pecan halves
1 egg	2 c. chopped candied fruit
1 tsp. vanilla	

Cream the butter and sugar together and add the egg and vanilla. Stir in the remaining ingredients. Chill for 1 hour. Divide dough in thirds and shape into 12-inch long rolls. Wrap in waxed paper and chill for 3 hours. Cut in 1/8-inch slices and place on ungreased cookie sheet. Bake at 325 degrees for 13 to 15 minutes.

Mrs. Silas Martin, Wilmington, Delaware

BLACK AND WHITE PINWHEELS

1 1/2 c. sifted flour	1 egg yolk
1/2 tsp. baking powder	3 tbsp. milk
1/8 tsp. salt	1/2 tsp. vanilla
1/2 c. shortening	1/2 pkg. semisweet chocolate
1/2 c. sugar	bits, melted

Sift the flour, baking powder and salt together. Cream the shortening and sugar together and add the egg yolk, milk and vanilla, mixing well. Add the flour mixture gradually and mix well. Divide the dough into 2 parts and add the melted chocolate to 1 part. Chill dough for about 30 minutes. Roll out each part separately between 2 sheets of waxed paper. Place chocolate dough on white dough and press together lightly. Roll as for a jelly roll. Chill for several hours. Cut into 1/8-inch slices and place on ungreased cookie sheet. Bake at 400 degrees for 5 to 8 minutes. 4 dozen.

Mary W. Nettleton, Teague, Texas

CHOCOLATE AND CHERRY BUTTER COOKIES

2 1/2 c. sifted flour
1 1/2 tsp. baking powder
1/2 tsp. salt
1 c. butter
1 1/2 c. sugar
1 egg

2 tsp. vanilla
1/2 c. chopped candied cherries
1/3 c. chopped pecans
1 sq. unsweetened chocolate,
   melted

Sift flour, baking powder and salt together. Cream the butter in a bowl and add sugar, a small amount at a time, creaming well after each addition. Add the egg and vanilla and beat until fluffy. Blend in sifted ingredients. Divide dough into 2 equal portions. Add cherries to half the dough and mix. Add pecans and chocolate to remaining dough and mix. Chill dough well. Shape each portion of dough into 2 rolls 12 inches long. Press 1 chocolate and 1 cherry roll together and wrap in waxed paper or plastic wrap. Repeat with remaining dough. Chill for several hours. Cut into 1/4-inch slices and place on ungreased baking sheet. Bake at 375 degrees for 10 minutes or until lightly browned. Chocolate and cherry portions may be wrapped and baked separately, if desired. 8 dozen.

FROSTED SOUR CREAM DROPS

3 1/4 c. sifted flour	2 eggs
1 tsp. salt	1 tbsp. vanilla
1/2 tsp. baking powder	1/2 tsp. almond extract
1/2 tsp. soda	1 c. sour cream
1 c. butter	Butter Frosting
1 1/2 c. sugar	Browned unblanched almonds (opt.)

Sift flour, salt, baking powder and soda together. Cream the butter and sugar in a bowl until light and fluffy. Beat in the eggs, vanilla and almond extracts. Add sifted ingredients alternately with sour cream and blend. Shape into roll and wrap in waxed paper. Chill overnight. Slice and place 2 inches apart on greased baking sheet. Bake in 375-degree oven for 10 to 12 minutes, then cool. Spread tops of cookies with Butter Frosting and top with almonds. About 6 dozen.

Butter Frosting

1/4 c. butter	1 tsp. vanilla
2 1/2 c. sifted confectioners' sugar	1/2 tsp. almond extract
Dash of salt	2 tbsp. (about) light cream

Cream the butter in a bowl and stir in remaining ingredients, adding enough cream for spreading consistency.

CHOCOLATE RIPPLE REFRIGERATOR COOKIES

1 c. flour	1/2 c. (packed) brown sugar
1/2 tsp. salt	1/2 c. sugar
1/2 tsp. soda	1 egg
1/2 c. shortening	1 tsp. vanilla

1/2 tsp. almond extract

1 c. rolled oats

1/2 c. chopped nuts

1 oz. chocolate, melted

Sift the flour, salt and soda together and add the shortening, sugars, egg and flavorings. Beat until smooth, then fold in oats and nuts. Add melted chocolate, stirring only enough to give a marbled effect. Shape into rolls and wrap in waxed paper. Chill for several hours or overnight. Slice 1/4 inch thick and place on baking sheet. Bake at 350 degrees for 10 to 12 minutes. 2 1/2 dozen.

Mrs. Patsy Whigham, Warner Robins, Georgia

SIX-IN-ONE COOKIES

1 c. butter

1/2 c. (packed) brown sugar

1/2 c. sugar

1 egg, beaten

1/2 tsp. vanilla

2 c. flour

1/2 tsp. soda

1/4 tsp. salt

1/2 sq. bitter chocolate, melted

1/4 c. shredded coconut

1/4 c. chopped raisins

1/4 c. chopped pecans

1/2 tsp. cinnamon

1/4 tsp. nutmeg

Cream the butter and add the sugars gradually. Beat until light and fluffy. Add the egg and vanilla and mix well. Sift the flour, soda and salt together and add to creamed mixture gradually, beating well after each addition. Divide dough into 6 portions and add the chocolate to 1 portion, coconut to another, raisins to another, pecans to one, cinnamon and nutmeg to another and leave the last portion plain. Shape each portion into a roll 1 3/4 inches in diameter. Wrap and freeze. Slice frozen dough 1/8 inch thick and place on cookie sheet. Bake at 375 degrees for 10 to 12 minutes.

Mrs. J. O. Barham, Midlothian, Texas

DATE-NUT ROLL COOKIES

1/2 c. butter

1/2 c. brown sugar

3/4 c. sugar

1/2 tsp. vanilla

1 egg

2 c. flour

1/4 tsp. soda

1   7 1/4-oz. package dates, chopped

1/8 tsp. salt

1 tsp. lemon juice

1 c. chopped nuts

Combine the butter, brown sugar and 1/2 cup sugar and beat until creamy. Add the vanilla and egg and mix well. Combine the flour and soda and add to the butter mixture, mixing well. Chill dough for 2 hours. Combine the remaining sugar, 1/3 cup water, dates, salt and lemon juice in a saucepan and bring to a boil, then simmer for 5 minutes. Stir in the nuts and cool. Roll dough into rectangle and spread date mixture evenly over dough. Roll up as for jelly roll and chill overnight. Slice and place on a greased cookie sheet. Bake for 10 to 12 minutes in 400-degree oven.

Mrs. R. T. Franklin, New Market, Tennessee

CINNAMON CRISPIES

2 c. flour	2 sticks butter or margarine
1 tsp. baking powder	1 egg, beaten
1/2 tsp. salt	Milk
Sugar	1 tbsp. cinnamon

Sift the flour, baking powder, salt and 1 tablespoon sugar together into a bowl. Cut in 1 stick margarine until mixture resembles coarse meal. Mix the egg with enough milk to make 3/4 cup liquid and stir into flour mixture. Place on a floured board and knead 25 times. Roll into a rectangle about 1/4 inch thick. Melt remaining butter and spread about 3 tablespoons on rectangle. Mix 1 1/2 cups sugar and cinnamon and sprinkle 1/4 cup over butter on rectangle. Roll as for jelly roll. Wrap in waxed paper and chill overnight. Cut into 1/4-inch slices. Dip into remaining butter, then into remaining sugar mixture. Place on lightly greased cookie sheet. Bake at 425 degrees for 7 to 10 minutes.

Mrs. D. G. Samford, Frederick, Maryland

DATE PINWHEEL COOKIES

3/4 c. pitted dates	1/4 tsp. salt
6 tbsp. sugar	2/3 c. butter or margarine
6 tbsp. water	1 1/4 c. (packed) brown sugar
1/4 c. chopped nuts	1 1/2 tsp. grated orange rind
2 tsp. lemon juice	1 egg
2 c. sifted flour	1 tbsp. vinegar
1/4 tsp. soda	

Combine the dates, sugar and water in a saucepan and cook for about 5 minutes or until thick. Remove from heat and add nuts and lemon juice. Cool. Sift the flour, soda and salt together. Cream the butter and brown sugar in a bowl. Add orange rind and beat in the egg and vinegar. Blend in dry ingredients. Chill for several hours or overnight. Roll out on floured surface into 10 x 15-inch rectangle. Spread with date mixture and roll as for jelly roll. Chill overnight. Slice 1/4 inch thick and place on greased cookie sheet. Bake at 375 degrees for 12 to 15 minutes. Cool on rack. 5 dozen.

Mrs. Mildred J. Wehman, Columbus, Texas

GUMDROP COOKIES

1 c. shortening	1 tsp. cinnamon
1 c. sugar	1 9-oz. package mincemeat
1 c. brown sugar	1 c. finely chopped walnuts
2 eggs	2/3 c. finely cut green and
2 1/2 c. sifted flour	red gumdrops
1 tsp. salt	Pecan halves
1/2 tsp. soda	

Combine shortening, sugars and eggs and cream thoroughly. Combine the dry ingredients and sift. Combine the mincemeat, walnuts and gumdrops and add 1/2 cup of the flour mixture, then mix until well coated. Stir the remaining flour mixture into the creamed mixture and mix well. Add the mincemeat mixture and blend well. Pack firmly into six 6-ounce frozen juice cans and freeze or chill for several hours. Cut in 1/8-inch slices and place 3/4 inch apart on ungreased cookie sheet. Top each cookie with pecan half. Bake at 375 degrees for 6 to 8 minutes. Cool slightly before removing from pan. 7-8 dozen.

Mrs. Andrew J. Taylor, Little Rock, Arkansas

SPICE SNAPS

1 3/4 c. sifted flour	1/8 tsp. ginger
1/2 tsp. soda	1/2 c. margarine
1/2 tsp. salt	3/4 c. sugar
1/4 tsp. cinnamon	1 egg white
1/8 tsp. cloves	Chocolate-flavored syrup

Sift flour, soda, salt and spices together. Cream the margarine and sugar in a bowl. Add the egg white and beat until light and fluffy. Add sifted ingredients and mix well. Shape into two 1 3/4-inch rolls. Wrap in waxed paper and chill for several hours or overnight. Slice 1/8 inch thick and place on a greased cookie sheet. Dip tines of a fork in the chocolate syrup and draw lightly across top of each cookie twice, making a waffle effect. Bake at 350 degrees for 8 to 10 minutes. About 3 dozen.

ICEBOX COOKIES

3 eggs	1/2 tsp. salt
1 c. butter, softened	1 tsp. soda
1 c. sugar	1 tsp. baking powder
4 c. sifted flour	1 tsp. vanilla

Beat the eggs until light, then add the butter and blend well. Add the sugar and beat until creamy. Sift the dry ingredients together and blend into the creamed mixture gradually. Stir in the vanilla. Shape into a roll and wrap in waxed paper. Chill for several hours or overnight. Slice and place on baking sheet. Bake at 400 degrees for 10 to 12 minutes or until light brown.

Mrs. Melvin Folmar, Huxford, Alabama

OLD-FASHIONED TEA CAKES

1 c. butter	1 tsp. nutmeg
1 c. sugar	3 1/2 c. flour
3 eggs	Cinnamon sugar

Cream the butter and sugar together, then add the eggs, nutmeg and flour. Beat until well mixed. Form the dough into three 2-inch thick rolls and wrap in waxed paper. Chill for 3 hours, then slice in 1/4-inch thick slices and place on baking sheet. Bake at 350 degrees for 10 minutes, then sprinkle with cinnamon sugar.

Kathryn Elwert, Wichita Falls, Texas

PECAN CRISPIES

1/2 c. shortening	1/8 tsp. salt
1 c. sugar	1 tsp. baking powder
1 well-beaten egg	1 c. chopped pecans
2 c. flour	

Cream the shortening and sugar together, then add the egg and beat well. Sift the dry ingredients together and add to the creamed mixture, mixing well. Stir in the pecans. Shape into a roll and wrap in waxed paper. Chill for several hours. Slice and place on a greased cookie sheet. Bake at 350 degrees for 12 to 15 minutes.

Lenna De Lony, Bradley, Arkansas

PEANUT COOKIES

1 c. shortening	1 tsp. cinnamon
1/2 c. peanut butter	1/4 tsp. cloves
2 c. (packed) brown sugar	1/4 tsp. nutmeg
3 eggs, well beaten	1 c. salted peanuts, chopped
4 c. all-purpose flour	fine

Cream the shortening until fluffy, then blend in the peanut butter. Add the sugar and the eggs, mixing well. Sift the dry ingredients together and add to the creamed mixture, mixing well. Stir in the peanuts and form into rolls. Wrap in waxed paper and refrigerate for several hours. Slice thin and place on cookie sheet. Bake at 425 degrees for 8 to 10 minutes. 150 cookies.

Mrs. U. G. Richmond, Walnut Grove, Mississippi

HIGHLAND FLINGS

1 6-oz. package semisweet chocolate morsels
1 c. butter or margarine
1 c. sugar
1 egg
3 tsp. vanilla

2 1/2 c. sifted all-purpose flour
1 1/4 tsp. baking powder
1/2 tsp. salt
1 c. rolled oats

Melt the chocolate morsels over hot, not boiling, water, then remove from water. Cream the butter, sugar, egg and vanilla in a bowl. Sift the flour, baking powder and salt together and stir into creamed mixture. Add the oats and mix well. Reserve 1 cup of the dough and chill. Add melted chocolate to remaining dough and chill until firm enough to handle. Roll out chocolate dough between 2 sheets of waxed paper to 10 x 18-inch rectangle, then peel off top sheet of paper. Roll out reserved light dough between 2 sheets of waxed paper to 8 x 18-inch rectangle and peel off top sheet of paper. Invert light dough on chocolate dough and remove paper. Roll from 18-inch edge as for a jelly roll. Wrap and chill for several hours. Cut in 1/4-inch slices and place 1 inch apart on ungreased cookie sheet. Bake in a 375-degree oven for 8 minutes. 6 dozen.

PEACH REFRIGERATOR COOKIES

3/4 c. butter	3 tsp. baking powder
1 1/2 c. (packed) dark brown sugar	1 tsp. salt
	1/4 c. milk
1 egg	1 c. chopped dried peaches
2 1/2 c. flour	1 c. chopped nuts

Cream the butter, sugar and egg together. Sift the dry ingredients together and add to the creamed mixture alternately with the milk. Add peaches and nuts and mix well. Shape into rolls and wrap in waxed paper, then place in freezer until ready to bake. Slice thin and place on baking sheet. Bake in 400-degree oven for 12 to 15 minutes.

Mrs. Stanley R. Smith, Doraville, Georgia

PECAN CRUNCHIES

2 c. melted butter or margarine	4 1/4 c. sifted flour
1 c. packed brown sugar	1 tsp. baking powder
1 c. sugar	1/2 tsp. salt
3 eggs, beaten	1 tsp. cinnamon
1/2 tsp. almond flavoring	1 c. chopped pecans

Combine the butter, sugars, eggs and almond flavoring and beat with electri mixer at medium speed for 3 minutes. Sift the dry ingredients together and add to the creamed mixture. Add pecans and mix at low speed until thoroughly mixed. Shape into long rolls and wrap in waxed paper, then chill for several hours. Slice thin and place on ungreased baking sheet. Bake at 400 degrees for 10 minutes. Dough may be kept for several weeks in refrigerator. 6 dozen.

Mrs. Albertine P. McKellar, Rowland, North Carolina

PECAN ICEBOX COOKIES

1 c. (packed) brown sugar	1/2 tsp. baking powder
1 c. sugar	3 c. flour
1 c. butter	1 c. chopped pecans
1 egg	

Cream the sugars and butter together, then add the egg and mix well. Stir in the remaining ingredients. Shape into a long roll about 2 inches in diameter and wrap in waxed paper. Place in refrigerator overnight. Slice and place on a baking sheet. Bake at 400 degrees until light brown. 5 dozen.

Mrs. A. K. King, Wharton, Texas

PECAN REFRIGERATOR COOKIES

1 c. butter or margarine	2 eggs, beaten
2 c. (packed) brown sugar	3 1/2 c. sifted flour

1 tsp. soda
1/2 tsp. salt

1 tsp. cream of tartar
1 c. chopped pecans

Cream the butter and sugar together, then add the eggs, mixing well. Sift the dry ingredients together and add to the butter mixture. Mix well. Add the pecans and stir until well mixed. Divide the mixture into 4 parts and shape each part into a roll, about 1 1/2 inches in diameter. Wrap in waxed paper and chill in refrigerator for at least 4 hours. Slice into 1/4-inch slices and place on ungreased cookie sheet. Bake for 8 minutes at 375 degrees. Remove from cookie sheet immediately. 12 dozen.

Jane Pate Rawson, Orange, Texas

ALMOND CRESCENTS

1/2 c. butter or margarine
1 c. sugar
6 tbsp. evaporated milk
3 eggs

1/2 tsp. salt
1 5/8 c. flour
Chopped almonds

Cream the butter and sugar in a bowl. Stir in the milk and 2 eggs. Add the salt and flour and mix well. Chill overnight. Roll out on a floured surface and cut in triangular shapes. Beat remaining egg and brush on triangles. Sprinkle with almonds. Place on a greased cookie sheet. Bake at 375 degrees until golden brown.

CRUNCHY FUDGE SANDWICHES

1 6-oz. package butterscotch
   morsels
	1/2 c. sifted confectioners'
	   sugar

1/2 c. peanut butter	2 tbsp. softened margarine
4 c. oven-toasted rice cereal	or butter
1 6-oz. package semisweet chocolate morsels	1 tbsp. water

Melt the butterscotch morsels and peanut butter in top of a double boiler over hot, not boiling, water and stir until blended. Remove from heat. Add the rice cereal and stir until coated with butterscotch mixture. Press 1/2 of the mixture in a buttered 8 x 8 x 2-inch pan and refrigerate until chilled. Reserve remaining cereal mixture. Melt the chocolate morsels, sugar, margarine and water in top of a double boiler over hot, not boiling, water. Spread over chilled cereal mixture and spread reserved cereal mixture over chocolate mixture. Press gently. Refrigerate until chilled. Remove from refrigerator about 10 minutes before cutting, then cut into 1 1/2-inch squares.

Photograph for this recipe on cover.

KRIS KRINGLES

1 c. sugar	1 6-oz. package semisweet
1 c. light corn syrup	chocolate morsels
1 c. peanut butter	1 6-oz. package butterscotch
6 c. oven-toasted rice cereal	morsels

Mix the sugar and corn syrup in a 3-quart saucepan and bring to a boil over moderate heat. Remove from heat. Stir in the peanut butter and cereal and press into buttered 13 x 9-inch pan. Let harden. Melt the chocolate and butterscotch morsels over hot, not boiling, water and stir until blended. Spread over cereal mixture and chill for about 5 minutes or until chocolate mixture is firm. Cut into diamonds, squares or bars. About 4 dozen.

Photograph for this recipe on page 1.

CHAUDRON COOKIES

1 c. sugar	1 c. graham cracker crumbs
1/2 c. evaporated milk	12 marshmallows, quartered
1/2 c. butter	1 c. chopped nuts

Combine the sugar, milk and butter in a saucepan and bring to a boil. Cook for 6 minutes, stirring constantly. Add the remaining ingredients and mix well. Drop onto waxed paper and cool for 10 minutes.

Nettie Baty, Collinsville, Texas

BOILED OATMEAL COOKIES

2 c. sugar	1 stick margarine or butter
4 tbsp. cocoa	1/2 c. milk

2 1/2 c. oatmeal
2 tsp. vanilla

1 c. grated coconut
1/2 c. chopped nuts

Combine the sugar, cocoa, margarine and milk and mix well. Bring to a boil and boil for 1 minute and 30 seconds, stirring constantly. Remove from heat and add the remaining ingredients. Stir until well blended, then drop by teaspoonfuls onto waxed paper and cool.

Jo Ann Reese, Thomson, Georgia

NUTMEG COOKIES

1/2 c. butter or margarine
1/2 c. sugar
6 tbsp. cream or milk
3 tbsp. orange juice
Grated rind of 1 orange

1 1/2 c. flour
2 c. potato flour
1 1/2 tsp. nutmeg
1/2 tsp. salt

Cream the butter and sugar in a bowl. Mix the cream, orange juice and orange rind. Sift the flours, nutmeg and salt together and add to the creamed mixture alternately with orange juice mixture. Shape into a roll and wrap in waxed paper. Refrigerate overnight. Slice and cut a hole in one side of each cookie. Place on a greased baking sheet. Bake at 375 degrees for 8 to 10 minutes.

BUTTERSCOTCHIES

1/2 c. evaporated milk
3/4 c. sugar
2 tbsp. butter or margarine
1 6-oz. package butterscotch
    morsels

1 tsp. vanilla
2 c. crisp ready-to-eat cereal
1 1/4 c. flaked coconut
1/2 c. coarsely chopped
    California walnuts

Combine the evaporated milk, sugar and butter in a 2-quart saucepan and bring to a boil, stirring constantly. Continue to boil, stirring constantly, for 2 minutes, then remove from heat. Add the butterscotch morsels and vanilla and stir until smooth. Add cereal, coconut and walnuts and mix until well coated. Drop quickly by rounded teaspoonfuls on a greased or waxed paper-lined sheet. Let stand until cool. 4 dozen.

Photograph for this recipe on page 5.

UNBAKED MINTED BROWNIES

1 c. chopped walnuts or pecans
2 c. miniature marshmallows
4 c. graham cracker crumbs
1 c. confectioners' sugar

2 6-oz. packages semisweet
    chocolate pieces
1 c. evaporated milk
3/4 tsp. peppermint extract

Mix the walnuts, marshmallows, graham cracker crumbs and confectioners' sugar in a large mixing bowl. Heat chocolate and evaporated milk in a small saucepan over low heat, stirring constantly, until smoothly blended. Remove from heat and stir in the peppermint extract. Reserve 1/2 cup of the chocolate mixture, then mix the remainder with the graham cracker mixture until all crumbs are moistened. Turn into a well-buttered 9 x 9 x 1 1/2-inch square pan and press down. Spread the reserved chocolate mixture on top and chill until ready to serve. Cut into 2-inch squares.

Photograph for this recipe on page 88.

NANAIMO COOKIES

Butter
1/4 c. sugar
5 tbsp. cocoa
1 tsp. vanilla
1 egg, beaten
2 c. graham cracker crumbs
1/2 c. chopped walnuts

1 c. flaked coconut
2 tbsp. instant vanilla
    pudding mix
3 tbsp. milk
2 c. powdered sugar
4 sq. semisweet chocolate

Combine 1/2 cup butter, sugar, cocoa and vanilla in top of double boiler and cook, stirring until well blended. Stir in the egg and cook for 5 minutes longer, stirring constantly. Add the crumbs, walnuts and coconut and mix well. Spread in a buttered 9-inch square pan and cool. Chill for 15 minutes. Cream 1/2 cup butter and beat in the pudding mix and milk. Add the powdered sugar and beat until smooth. Spread over the cooled layer, then chill for 15 minutes longer.

Melt the chocolate and 1 tablespoon butter together over low heat, then spread over powdered sugar mixture. Chill and cut into squares to serve.

Mrs. Barbara Garrett, Pine Bluff, Arkansas

CANDIED COOKIES

2 c. sugar
1/2 c. milk
1 stick butter or margarine
4 tbsp. cocoa

2 1/2 c. quick-cooking oats
1/4 c. chopped nuts
2 tsp. vanilla
1/2 c. peanut butter

Combine the sugar, milk, butter and cocoa in a saucepan and bring to a boil. Cook for 1 minute and 30 seconds, stirring constantly. Remove from heat and add remaining ingredients. Beat until mixture is well blended. Drop by teaspoonfuls onto waxed paper. Cool and serve. 50 cookies.

Faye Quinley, Corsicana, Texas

CHOCOLATE BALLS

3/4 c. margarine
3/4 c. confectioners' sugar
2 c. rolled oats

3 tbsp. cocoa
1 tsp. vanilla

Cream the margarine with the sugar. Stir in the oats, cocoa and vanilla. Shape into balls. May be rolled in sugar, flaked coconut, roasted almonds or crumbled corn flakes. Refrigerate until chilled.

CHOCOLATE DELIGHTS

Vanilla wafer crumbs	4 eggs
1 c. butter, softened	3/4 tsp. peppermint flavoring
2 c. sifted powdered sugar	2 tsp. vanilla
4 sq. bitter chocolate, melted	

Place 1 1/2 teaspoons crumbs in each of 24 paper baking cups. Cream the butter until fluffy and beat in the sugar gradually. Add the chocolate, eggs and the flavorings and beat well. Spoon into the paper cups and top each with 1 1/2 teaspoons crumbs. Cool and serve.

Mrs. Claude Neil, Farmersville, Texas

COOKIE DELIGHTS

1 lge. package chocolate bits	1 can Chinese noodles
1 lge. package butterscotch bits	

Melt the chocolate and butterscotch pieces in top of double boiler over hot water. Remove from heat and stir in the noodles. Drop by teaspoonfuls onto waxed paper and cool.

Mrs. Otto Murphy, Springfield, Tennessee

DATE BALLS

1 pkg. dates, chopped	1 tsp. vanilla
1 c. chopped nuts	1/2 c. cream or evaporated milk
18 marshmallows, chopped	2 c. graham cracker crumbs

Combine the dates, nuts and marshmallows and add the vanilla to the milk. Combine all the ingredients except the crumbs. Shape into small balls and roll in the crumbs. 30-50 balls.

Mrs. Newton V. Colston, Martinsville, Virginia

FUDGE COOKIES

3 c. quick-cooking oats	1/2 c. cocoa
1 tsp. vanilla	1/2 c. evaporated milk
1 c. chopped pecans or coconut	1 stick margarine
2 c. sugar	

Combine the oatmeal, vanilla and pecans in a large bowl. Combine the sugar, cocoa and milk in a large saucepan and bring to a full boil, stirring constantly. Add the margarine and stir until melted. Add the oats mixture and stir until well combined. Drop by teaspoonfuls onto waxed paper and cool.

Mrs. Robert Alterkamp, Comfort, Texas

HONEY SLICES

1 1/2 c. powdered milk	1 can coconut
1 c. honey	1 c. whole wheat flakes
1 c. peanut butter	

Combine the powdered milk, honey and peanut butter and stir until thoroughly mixed. Shape into long rolls. Mix the coconut and wheat flakes together on waxed paper and roll the rolls in mixture until well coated. Cut in slices and chill.

Janie Haneline, Cumberland Furnace, Tennessee

ORANGE-COCONUT BALLS

1 6-oz. can frozen orange juice	1 stick melted margarine
	1/2 to 3/4 c. chopped nuts
1 lge. box vanilla wafers, crushed	1 box powdered sugar
	Coconut

Combine all of the ingredients except the coconut. Mix well and shape into balls. Roll the balls in the coconut until well coated.

Mrs. Hal J. Wallis, Dallas, Texas

PEANUT BUTTER-OATMEAL COOKIES

1/4 c. butter or margarine	1/2 c. milk
3 c. sugar	1/2 c. peanut butter
4 tbsp. cocoa	3 c. rolled oats

Combine the butter, sugar, cocoa and milk in saucepan and cook, stirring constantly, over high heat for 5 minutes. Remove from heat and add the peanut butter and oats, mixing well. Drop by teaspoonfuls onto waxed paper and cool. 4 dozen.

Edna B. Smith, Georgiana, Alabama

SWEET TOOTH TREATS

1/2 c. butter	1 c. malted cereal granules
2/3 c. sugar	1 9-oz. can crushed pineapple
2 eggs, well-beaten	1 7 1/4-oz. box vanilla wafers
1 c. chopped pecans	

Cream the butter and sugar together, then add the eggs, pecans, cereal and pineapple with juice. Crush the wafers into fine crumbs. Alternate layers of crumbs and pineapple mixture in 8-inch square pan, starting and ending with crumbs. Chill at least 8 hours. Cut into squares.

Mrs. Sam Keith, Franklin, North Carolina

cookies for small cooks

It sometimes seems that no one loves cookie making quite so much as children. Say you are going to bake cookies – or even hint at it – and immediately there is a throng of eager "helpers" around you. Baking cookies is fun for children of all ages . . . and a wonderful way to introduce fledgling cooks to the principles of good cooking!

This section is full of easy-to-prepare, fun-to-eat cookie recipes of every description designed especially for small cooks. If it's holiday time and your children's creations will decorate the tree, try rolled Sugar Cookies. Monkey Face Cookies are drop cookies that are as much fun to prepare as to eat. Then there are the filled cookies so beloved by children, like the Jelly Cookies and Cowboy Pies you'll find in this section.

When it's the children's turn in the kitchen, you become the helper. Assist them in reading the recipe and assembling all the ingredients they'll need. Turn on the oven and make a general rule that no one is to go near it. Wash hands all around, clip back long, loose hair, distribute aprons or old shirts, then watch the fun! And when the cooking excitement is over, why not plan a tea party so they can enjoy the delicious cookies they have created.

For those special occasions when it's your small cook's time in the kitchen, this is the section you can rely on for children-perfect recipes – every time!

BANANA-OATMEAL COOKIES

2 bananas, mashed	2/3 c. margarine, melted
1 c. crushed peanuts	1 tsp. vanilla
2/3 c. brown sugar	1 1/2 c. quick-cooking oats
2 eggs, beaten	1 1/2 c. flour

Combine all ingredients and mix thoroughly. Drop by teaspoonfuls onto lightly greased baking sheet. Bake at 400 degrees for about 7 minutes or until brown.

Mrs. Minnie Pennington, Northport, Alabama

COCONUT FINGERS

1 c. (packed) brown sugar	2 c. chopped dates
2 eggs	1 c. chopped nuts
1 tsp. vanilla	2 c. grated coconut

Combine the brown sugar, eggs and vanilla and beat well. Add the dates and nuts and mix thoroughly. Drop the dough by heaping teaspoonfuls into the coconut and roll like fingers. Place on ungreased cookie sheet. Bake at 350 degrees for 10 to 12 minutes or until golden brown. 2 dozen.

Mrs. Ray Leggitt, Carthage, Missouri

RAISIN CRUNCHIES

1/2 c. shortening	1/2 tsp. salt
1/2 c. sugar	1/4 c. evaporated milk
1 egg	1 c. raisins
Grated rind of 1 orange	1/2 c. broken nuts
1 c. flour	3 c. corn flakes
1 1/2 tsp. baking powder	

Cream the shortening and sugar, then add the egg and orange rind. Beat briskly. Sift the flour with the baking powder and salt and add half the flour mixture to the sugar mixture. Mix thoroughly, then blend in the milk. Add the remaining flour and mix well. Stir in the raisins, nuts and corn flakes. Drop by teaspoonfuls onto greased cookie sheet. Bake in 350-degree oven for about 15 minutes.

Mrs. Kelly Jones, Warrior, Alabama

CAROUSEL AND ANIMALS

1 c. sugar	1 tbsp. lemon extract
1/2 c. shortening	3 1/2 c. flour
2 eggs	2 tsp. baking powder
2 tbsp. milk	

Cookies For Small Cooks

Cream the sugar and shortening in a bowl until light and fluffy. Add the eggs, milk and lemon extract and beat well. Sift remaining ingredients together and add to creamed mixture. Cover and chill. Roll out on a floured surface to 1/4-inch thickness and cut with animal cookie cutters. Place on a lightly greased baking sheet. Bake at 375 degrees for 8 minutes or until lightly browned.

Carousel

3 c. sugar	3/4 c. water
1 1/2 c. light corn syrup	6 5 1/2-in. dowel sticks

Line two 9-inch round cake pans with aluminum foil, letting foil extend beyond rim. Combine the sugar, corn syrup and water in a heavy saucepan. Cook over low heat, stirring constantly until sugar is completely dissolved. Cook over medium-low heat, without stirring, to 295 degrees on a candy thermometer or until a small amount dropped into cold water separates into threads which are hard. Pour immediately into prepared pans, about 2/3 of the mixture into 1 pan and 1/3 of the mixture into the other. Let set for about 5 minutes. Stand dowel sticks upright in thickest candy, equal distances around edge of pan, alternately 1 inch and 2 inches from edge. Support sticks with hands for several seconds or until firm, if necessary. Sticks must be straight and tops even to support top of carousel. Let set until candy layer is cold and hard. Lift from pan, using ends of foil, then remove foil. Place on a flat plate. Place animal cookies against sticks and decorate carousel with ribbon, if desired. Balance an empty layer cake pan on top of sticks to test arrangement, then balance remaining candy layer on sticks.

CORN FLAKE MACAROONS

2 tbsp. butter or margarine	1 c. coconut
1/3 c. evaporated milk	1 1/2 c. corn flakes
3/4 c. sugar	1/2 c. chopped nuts (opt.)
1/2 tsp. vanilla	

Combine the butter, milk and sugar in a saucepan and bring to a boil. Cook over medium heat for 2 minutes, stirring frequently. Remove from heat, then stir in the remaining ingredients, mixing well. Drop from teaspoon onto waxed paper and cool.

Barbara Ellen Shore, Walnut Cove, North Carolina

MONKEY FACE COOKIES

1 egg	1 tsp. soda
1 c. sugar	1/2 tsp. salt
2 tbsp. shortening, melted	1 tsp. vanilla
1/4 c. sour milk	Raisins
2 c. sifted flour	

Combine the egg, sugar, shortening and sour milk and mix well. Sift the dry ingredients together and add gradually to creamed mixture. Stir in the vanilla. Drop from a teaspoon onto a greased cookie sheet, then place 3 raisins on each cookie for eyes and nose. Bake at 350 degrees for 8 to 10 minutes. 3 dozen.

Mrs. Bobbie Hemphill, Miami, Florida

VANILLA WAFER COOKIES

1 stick margarine	2 c. vanilla wafer crumbs
2 c. sugar	1 c. grated coconut
1 sm. can evaporated milk	1 c. chopped nuts

Combine the margarine, sugar and milk in a saucepan and cook to a soft-ball stage. Remove from heat and add the remaining ingredients immediately. Mix well, then drop from spoon quickly onto waxed paper and cool. 2 dozen.

Mrs. Ruth Moon, Nashville, Tennessee

STIR AND DROP COOKIES

2 eggs	3/4 c. sugar
2/3 c. cooking oil	2 c. self-rising flour
Grated rind of 1 lemon	Pecan halves
2 tsp. vanilla	

Beat the eggs with a fork until well mixed, then add the oil, lemon rind and vanilla and blend. Add the sugar and mix well, then stir in the flour. Drop by teaspoonfuls onto ungreased cookie sheet. Flatten with greased glass dipped in additional sugar. Decorate with pecan halves. Bake at 400 degrees for about 10 minutes or until light brown.

Martha Turner, Carrolton, Georgia

GOLDEN CHOCOLATE BROWNIES

1 pkg. brownie mix	1 6-oz. package chocolate
1/2 c. chopped nuts	pieces
16 lge. marshmallows	2 tbsp. butter

Prepare the brownie mix according to package directions and blend in the nuts. Bake according to package directions. Cover brownies immediately with marshmallows and return to oven to melt. Spread evenly over top of brownies. Melt the chocolate with the butter and spread over marshmallows. Cool and cut into squares. Marshmallow creme may be used instead of marshmallows. 16 brownies.

Mary K. Love, Miami, Florida

SUGAR COOKIES

2 c. sifted flour	1 egg
1 1/4 tsp. baking powder	Milk
1/4 tsp. salt	3/4 c. sugar
1/3 c. corn oil	1 tsp. vanilla

Sift the flour, baking powder and salt together into a mixing bowl. Add the corn oil and blend well. Mixture will appear dry. Beat the egg, add enough milk to make 1/3 cup liquid and stir in the sugar and vanilla. Beat until very light and fluffy, then stir into the flour mixture. Chill for about 1 hour. Roll out 1/8 to 1/4 inch thick on a floured board or cloth and cut with a floured 2-inch round cutter or as desired. Place on an ungreased cookie sheet. Bake in 400-degree oven for about 9 minutes or until lightly browned. May be sprinkled with colored sugar before baking, if desired. 3 dozen 2-inch cookies.

CRISP PEANUT BUTTER COOKIES

1 c. margarine
1 c. creamy or chunk-style
  peanut butter
1 c. sugar
1 c. (firmly packed) brown sugar
2 eggs, beaten

1 tsp. vanilla
2 1/2 c. sifted flour
1 tsp. baking powder
1 tsp. soda
1 tsp. salt

Mix the margarine, peanut butter and sugars in a bowl until blended, then beat in the eggs and vanilla. Sift flour, baking powder, soda and salt together and stir into sugar mixture until well blended. Chill, if needed. Shape into 1-inch balls. Place about 2 inches apart on a greased baking sheet and flatten with floured bottom of glass or with floured fork making crosswise pattern. Bake in 350-degree oven for 12 to 15 minutes or until lightly browned. Place 2 cookies together, using additional peanut butter as filling, to make cookie sandwiches. Follow recipe for Crisp Peanut Butter Cookies to make jelly thumb print cookies, pressing small indentation into each ball of dough with thumb instead of flattening. Remove from baking sheet while warm and press again with thumb. Cool and fill each indentation with jelly or jam. 6 dozen single cookies.

JELLY COOKIES

3/4 c. shortening
2/3 c. sugar
1 egg
1 tsp. vanilla

1 tsp. almond extract
2 c. flour
1/2 tsp. baking powder
Jelly

Cream the shortening and sugar and add the egg, vanilla and almond extract. Add the flour and baking powder and beat at medium speed of electric mixer until well blended. Drop from a teaspoon onto ungreased cookie sheet. Make a slight indentation in center of each cookie and fill with jelly. Bake for 15 minutes at 350 degrees. 3 dozen.

Mrs. Lucille Smith, Knoxville, Tennessee

112

COWBOY PIES

1/2 c. soft butter	1 1/2 tsp. soda
1 c. sugar	2 tsp. salt
1 egg	1/2 c. milk
2 c. flour	1/2 c. cocoa
1/2 tsp. baking powder	1 tsp. vanilla

Cream the butter and sugar, then add the egg and beat thoroughly. Sift the flour with the baking powder, soda and salt and add with the milk and cocoa to creamed mixture. Beat thoroughly and add the vanilla. Drop by spoonfuls onto cookie sheet. Bake at 400 degrees for 7 minutes. Cool.

Filling

1/2 c. shortening	4 tsp. milk
2 c. powdered sugar	1 tsp. vanilla
1 c. marshmallow creme	

Combine all ingredients and mix thoroughly. Spread between 2 cookies.

Kay Mills, Virginia Beach, Virginia

CHRISTMAS COOKIES

2 1/3 c. sifted flour	2/3 c. sugar
1/2 tsp. salt	1 egg
1 c. margarine	1 tsp. vanilla

Sift the flour and salt together. Mix the margarine and sugar in a bowl until blended. Add the egg and vanilla and beat well. Stir in the flour mixture and chill for about 1 hour or until dough may be handled. Roll out, 1/3 at a time, to 1/8-inch thickness on lightly floured board or cloth. Cut as desired with cookie cutters and place on a greased cookie sheet. Bake in 400-degree oven for 6 to 7 minutes or until lightly browned on edges. Cool and decorate as desired. 3 dozen 2-inch cookies.

Photograph for this recipe on page 106.

PRIZE WINNER ICEBOX COOKIES

1/2 c. butter or margarine	1 3/4 c. sifted flour
1 c. sugar	1/2 tsp. baking powder
2 tsp. vanilla	1/2 tsp. salt
1 egg	1 c. chopped nuts

Cream the butter and sugar and add the vanilla and egg. Beat until blended. Sift the dry ingredients together and add the nuts. Add to the sugar mixture gradually, stirring well after each addition. Shape in a long roll, 2 inches in diameter, and wrap in waxed paper. Chill in refrigerator overnight. Slice 1/8 to 1/4 inch thick and place on cookie sheet. Bake at 400 degrees for 7 minutes. 4-5 dozen.

Mrs. Cliff Winstead, Union, Mississippi

CUT-OUT COOKIES

3 c. sifted flour	1 c. margarine
1 c. sugar	2 eggs, slightly beaten
1/2 tsp. baking powder	1 1/2 tsp. almond extract

Sift the flour, sugar and baking powder together into a mixing bowl and cut in the margarine until mixture resembles fine crumbs. Stir in the eggs and almond extract until smooth, then chill. Roll out, 1/3 at a time, to 1/8-inch thickness on floured board and cut into desired shapes. Place on ungreased cookie sheet. Bake in 375-degree oven for 8 to 10 minutes or until edges are very lightly browned. Jumbo spice cookies may be made by using firmly packed brown sugar instead of sugar, adding 1 1/2 teaspoons cinnamon, 1/2 to 1 teaspoon ginger, 1/2 teaspoon cloves and 1/2 teaspoon nutmeg with dry ingredients and omitting almond extract. 5 dozen 2-inch or 1 1/2 dozen 5-inch cookies.

Photograph for this recipe on page 106.

DECORATOR'S FROSTING

1 c. margarine	Food colorings
1 lb. confectioners' sugar, sifted	

Mix the margarine and confectioners' sugar in a bowl, beating until smooth. Divide into separate bowls and tint as desired. Press frosting through decorating tube to decorate cookies. Blend in several drops of water if frosting becomes too stiff. 3 1/4 cups.

Photograph for this recipe on page 106.

COOKIE GLAZE

3/4 c. sugar	3 c. confectioners' sugar
1/3 c. water	2 tsp. lemon juice (opt.)
2 tbsp. light corn syrup	Food colorings (opt.)

Mix the sugar, water and corn syrup in a small saucepan. Cook over medium heat, stirring constantly, until mixture comes to a boil. Remove from heat and cool for about 5 minutes. Add confectioners' sugar gradually, beating until smooth after each addition, then stir in the lemon juice. Divide into separate bowls and tint desired colors for colored glaze. 1 1/4 cups.

Photograph for this recipe on page 106.

NOEL COOKIE PLAQUE

Roll out Cut-Out Cookie dough 1/4 inch thick and cut round cookies 4 3/4 inches in diameter. Bake as directed. Cool and cover with white Cookie Glaze. Let set until hardened. Make large script letters to spell out NOEL on 4 cookies, using green-tinted Decorator's Frosting run through a pastry tube. Trim edges of cookies with red tinted Decorator's Frosting. Let set until hardened. Attach cookies to a board, heavy paper board or a 24 1/2 x 7-inch tray with any household glue. Do not eat cookies.

Photograph for this recipe on page 106.

GINGER COOKIES

5 c. sifted flour	3 tsp. ginger
1 tsp. soda	2/3 c. butter
1 tsp. salt	1 c. sugar
1 tsp. cinnamon	1 c. dark molasses
1 tsp. nutmeg	2 eggs, beaten

Sift flour, soda, salt and spices together. Cream the butter in a bowl. Add the sugar and beat until light and fluffy. Blend in molasses and eggs. Add sifted ingredients and mix well. Chill in refrigerator for several hours or overnight. Roll out on lightly floured board or pastry cloth to 1/8-inch thickness. Cut with floured cookie cutters and place on greased baking sheet. Bake at 375 degrees for 10 to 12 minutes, then cool on rack. Decorate with buttercream frosting and cookie decorations, if desired. 4 dozen.

ORANGE SUGAR COOKIES

5 1/2 c. sifted flour	2 c. sugar
2 tsp. baking powder	4 eggs
2 tsp. salt	2 tbsp. grated orange rind
1 1/2 c. butter	

Sift flour, baking powder and salt together. Cream the butter in a bowl. Add the sugar and beat until light and fluffy. Blend in eggs and grated rind. Add sifted ingredients and mix well. Chill in refrigerator for several hours or overnight. Roll out on lightly floured board or pastry cloth to 1/8-inch thickness and cut with a floured cookie cutter. Place on ungreased baking sheet and sprinkle with additional sugar. Bake at 400 degrees for 6 to 8 minutes or until done and delicately browned, then cool on rack. Decorate with buttercream frosting and cookie decorations, if desired. 8 dozen.

SANTA'S TRAIN

6 c. sifted flour	1/2 c. sugar
1/4 tsp. salt	1 tsp. lemon extract
1 1/2 c. margarine	1 tsp. vanilla
1 c. light corn syrup	Frosting

Sift the flour and salt together. Cream the margarine in a bowl and add corn syrup and sugar, beating until well blended. Add flavorings, then sifted ingredients and mix thoroughly. Chill for several hours or overnight. Study picture. Divide dough into quarters. Roll out each of 3 quarters on a cookie sheet to rectangle 12 x 9 inches and 1/4 inch thick. Place on ungreased cookie sheet. Bake in 400-degree oven for 8 to 10 minutes or until edges are lightly browned. Cool on wire rack, then remove from cookie sheet. Roll remaining dough to 1/4-inch thickness on floured board. Cut out two 3-inch circles for wheels of locomotive and four 2-inch circles for wheels of other cars. Cut small oblong pieces for packages from remaining dough. Place on ungreased cookie sheet and bake for 8 to 10 minutes longer. Cut cardboard rectangles slightly smaller than the 3 large cookies, then attach to backs with corn syrup or frosting. Trace train outlines on these cookies with frosting, following pattern, using a medium writing tube, then add remaining details. Decorate wheels and packages, then attach to train with Frosting. Assemble train by propping pieces upright against colored poster board or foil-covered cardboard.

Frosting

2 tbsp. warm water	Food coloring
2 c. sifted confectioners' sugar	

Blend water into confectioners' sugar in a bowl. Add several drops additional water, if necessary, for desired consistency. Tint as desired.

116

BUTTERSCOTCH CHIP COOKIES

1/2 c. butter	1 tsp. soda
1 c. brown sugar	1 6-oz. package butterscotch
1 c. sugar	pieces
2 eggs, beaten	2 c. crushed potato chips
2 1/4 c. flour	

Cream the butter and the sugars, then add the eggs and mix well. Add the remaining ingredients and mix well. Roll in balls the size of a walnut and place on baking sheet. Bake for 12 minutes at 350 degrees. 3 dozen.

Mrs. Marsha Glenn, Beaufort, South Carolina

NUT SNOWBALLS

6 tbsp. sugar	2 tsp. vanilla
1 1/2 sticks butter or	2 1/2 c. flour
margarine	1 c. crushed pecans
2 tbsp. ice water	Powdered sugar

Cream the sugar and butter, then add the remaining ingredients except powdered sugar to form a stiff dough. Shape into bite-sized balls and place on a baking sheet. Bake at 300 degrees for about 20 minutes. Cool and roll in powdered sugar. 20 servings.

Mrs. Gordon M. Williams, Godwin, North Carolina

CINNAMON BALLS

1 stick soft butter	1 c. chopped pecans
3 tbsp. powdered sugar	Cinnamon sugar
1 c. sifted flour	

Cream the butter and blend in the sugar and flour. Stir in the pecans. Roll into small balls and place on a baking sheet. Bake at 375 degrees for about 10 minutes. Remove from baking sheet and dip in cinnamon sugar. 30 cookies.

Sandra Collins, Ocala, Florida

SNICKERDOODLES

1 1/2 c. sugar	2 tsp. cream of tartar
1 c. shortening	1 tsp. soda
2 eggs	1/2 tsp. salt
2 3/4 c. sifted flour	Cinnamon sugar

Cream the sugar, shortening and eggs. Sift the flour, cream of tartar, soda and salt together and add to creamed mixture. Mix until well blended, then chill for about 1 hour. Form into small balls the size of small walnuts and roll in the cinnamon sugar. Place on an ungreased cookie sheet about 2 inches apart. Bake at 425 degrees for 8 to 10 minutes. Cool before removing from cookie sheet. 90 cookies.

Ruby Logston, Pine Bluff, Arkansas

Candy is almost everyone's favorite snack — and with good reason. Every food the body takes in must be converted to sugar before it can be absorbed. Because candy *is* sugar, the conversion process is unnecessary, and the sugar from candy moves quickly to re-energize the body. It's no wonder that candy is such a popular between-meals snack.

Homemade candy is fun to make, as generations of homemakers know. It does take the right equipment and some careful watching, but when the result is a perfect pan of fudge, just-right chewy caramels, or a snap, cracking peanut brittle, the work is well worth it.

EQUIPMENT

To make candy, you'll need a large kettle and a double boiler, both common pieces of household equipment you probably already have on hand. Rubber

general directions
FOR SUCCESSFUL CANDY MAKING

spatulas, graduated measuring cups and spoons, and a set of wooden spoons are all inexpensive items which are great aids for successful candy making.

Add to these utensils a piece of marble. Most furniture manufacturers or marble quarries have pieces the size you'll need — about 30 inches square — for just a few dollars. This marble can be used not only for candy making but for rolling out pie crusts or kneading dough. It's a wonderful investment for an efficient kitchen.

You'll also want a candy thermometer to determine temperatures of your candies as they cook. A copper thermometer with a removable scale is easily cleaned after use.

Some of the equipment you'll need comes from candy supply houses. Rubber molds for chocolates, a depositing funnel and stick for wafers, dipping paper, crinkled paper candy cups, and lollypop sticks can all be bought economically from your nearest candy supply house. Just look in the yellow pages, or, if there isn't one listed in your directory, ask the local candy shop owner or baker where he buys his equipment.

CHOCOLATES

Chocolate for candy making is usually sold in blocks and must be tempered before you can use it. To temper chocolate, break it up in small pieces with an ice pick or an awl. Melt the pieces in the top part of a double boiler, being careful to keep the hot water at between 140 and 150 degrees (nicely warm to the touch). The addition of a lump of cocoa butter about the size of a walnut helps ensure smooth, glossy chocolate. Stir the melted chocolate thoroughly and carefully and avoid incorporating too much air.

When you are dipping candies in this chocolate, wait until it reaches a temperature of about 85 degrees — or feels slightly cool. Pick up the center, dip it, and pull up the chocolate. Still holding the candy with your fingertips, knock the back of your hand against a marble slab and excess chocolate should fall off. Squeeze the chocolate slightly and place it on the slab to set. If the candies sag and the chocolate coating forms a ring around the center as it sets, you have not removed enough chocolate. If the center shows through, you did not dip it enough. But a little practice will transform you into an expert chocolate maker!

FONDANT

Fondant is often used for chocolate centers. It is basically a sugar-milk-butter mixture prepared over very high heat. Mix the sugar and liquid before placing your pan over the flame. Use high heat and stir constantly until the mixture boils, and stir often after that. At 236 degrees on your candy thermometer (see the chart that follows for cold water test instructions), remove from heat. Let the mixture set until the dent made by a fingerprint fills only slowly.

Fondant is worked back and forth until it turns white and becomes less sticky. Two knives are usually used for this kneading process. After you have worked it for a few minutes, the fondant suddenly will become almost rock-hard. At this point, knead it with your hands until it is lumpless and almost semi-liquid. Now you have fondant ready to be coated with chocolate, made into bonbons, or used in any other confection you want to prepare. You may store leftover fondant in a bowl in your refrigerator. The bowl should be covered with a damp towel or piece of plastic wrap, and this covering should be changed every few days.

COLD WATER TEST/TEMPERATURE CHART

TYPES OF CANDY	COLD WATER TEST	TEMPERATURE AT SEA LEVEL * (in degrees as measured on candy thermometer)
Fudge, fondant	Soft ball (flattens when picked up)	234 — 240
Caramels	Firm ball (holds shape unless pressed)	240 — 248
Divinity, taffy	Hard ball (holds shape but is still pliable)	250 — 268
Butterscotch, English toffee	Soft crack (separated into hard threads that are not brittle)	270 — 290

*Subtract approximately two degrees for every 1,000 feet increase in altitude.

beaten, dipped & drop candies

Beaten, dipped, and drop candies are among those most often prepared — and with good reason. Candies like fudge, penuche, and divinity are popular favorites at every gathering . . . and they're remarkably easy to prepare.

Southern homemakers — who serve their best candies at church bazaars and suppers as well as at home — have created many delicious candy recipes. These are painstakingly developed recipes with just the right combination of ingredients to achieve a not-too-sweet but oh-so-good taste. Such recipes that are the pride and joy of the women who now share them with you in these pages.

Here you'll find recipes for many different kinds of that family favorite candy, fudge! Butter-Rum Fudge, Honey Fudge, Marshmallow Creme Fudge, and Vanilla Fudge are just four of the recipes awaiting you. There is a simple recipe for Chocolate-Covered Cherries — you can't imagine how fast they'll sell at your next bake sale! And just look at the recipe for Pastel Divinity — an old favorite that takes on new excitement when it appears in pale yellow, pink, or green colors.

The next time you're looking for a spectacularly different candy recipe, turn to this section. You're certain to find just the one you want among these home-tested beaten and drop candy recipes!

CHOCO-MINT SLICES

4 c. sugar
Dash of salt
1 tall can evaporated milk
2 6-oz. packages semisweet
   chocolate pieces

1 7 1/2-oz. jar marshmallow
   creme
1/2 tsp. peppermint extract
1 c. finely chopped pecans

Mix the sugar, salt and evaporated milk in a large saucepan. Cook and stir over low heat until sugar is dissolved. Bring to a rolling boil over medium heat, then cook for 7 minutes, stirring constantly. Remove from heat and add chocolate pieces, marshmallow creme and peppermint extract. Beat until smooth, then cool thoroughly. Divide into 3 parts. Shape each part into a roll about 12 inches long and roll in pecans to coat. Wrap in waxed paper and store in refrigerator until chilled. Slice and serve. About 3 1/2 pounds.

CARAMEL SQUARES

2 c. sugar
1 c. milk
4 tbsp. butter or margarine

1 tsp. vanilla
1/4 c. flaked coconut

Place 1 1/4 cups sugar and milk in a saucepan and place over moderate heat. Place remaining sugar in iron skillet and heat until melted, stirring constantly. Add to milk mixture and cook, stirring frequently, until small amount of mixture forms a firm ball in cold water. Remove from heat. Add the butter and beat until firm. Add the vanilla and coconut and pour into a well-buttered dish. Cool and cut in squares.

Mrs. Paul Glenn, Decatur, Alabama

GELATIN DIVINITY SQUARES

3 c. sugar
3/4 c. light corn syrup
3/4 c. water
2 egg whites, stiffly beaten

1 3-oz. package flavored
gelatin
1 c. chopped pecans

Combine the sugar, corn syrup and water in a saucepan and bring to a boil, stirring constantly. Reduce heat and cook to hard-ball stage, stirring occasionally. Combine the egg whites and gelatin in a bowl and beat until mixture forms stiff peaks. Pour hot syrup into egg white mixture in a thin stream, beating constantly, and beat until candy loses gloss and holds shape. Fold in the pecans. Pour into greased pan and cut in squares.

Mrs. W. W. Zeigler, Walterboro, South Carolina

PENUCHE

2 c. (packed) brown sugar
3/4 c. milk
1 tsp. vanilla

1 c. chopped nuts
2 tbsp. butter

Mix the sugar and milk in a saucepan and bring to a boil. Reduce heat and cook, stirring constantly, until small amount of mixture forms a soft ball when placed in cold water. Remove from heat and add vanilla, nuts and butter, beat until creamy and thick and pour into a greased pan. Cut into squares when firm.

Sara Judith Pitts, Century, Florida

ORANGE CARAMEL FUDGE

1 lge. orange
4 c. sugar
1 tall can evaporated milk

1/4 c. butter
1 c. chopped walnuts

Pare rind from the orange with very small layer of white. Cut rind into thin strips, then into very small pieces and set aside. Place 1 cup sugar in a very large, deep aluminum skillet. Place remaining sugar, evaporated milk and butter in a heavy 3-quart aluminum saucepan. Place skillet over very low heat to warm sugar and skillet. Cook the sugar mixture in saucepan over medium heat, stirring frequently, until sugar is dissolved. Cook, stirring occasionally, for 25 minutes or to 234 degrees on candy thermometer. Remove from heat. Increase heat under the sugar in skillet to medium and stir until sugar is completely melted and golden brown. Remove skillet from heat and place on wooden board. Stir in the cooked sugar mixture gradually, blending thoroughly. Temperature of sugar mixture will still be around 234 degrees. Mixture may look separated but will blend in smoothly. Add orange rind and walnuts to mixture in skillet and beat until mixture begins to stiffen and has fudge-like appearance. Mixture will be stiff and hot, but pliable. Turn into a lightly greased 8-inch square pan and spread evenly with spatula. Cool thoroughly, then cut into squares. About 2 pounds.

Photograph for this recipe on page 120.

PEANUT CREAMS

2 c. (firmly packed) light brown sugar	Pinch of salt
	1 c. chopped peanuts
3/4 c. hot water	3 tbsp. butter or margarine

Combine the sugar, water and salt in a saucepan and stir over low heat until sugar is dissolved. Cook to 236 degrees on candy thermometer or until small amount of mixture dropped in cold water forms a soft ball. Remove from the heat and cool to 110 degrees or until candy is lukewarm. Place the peanuts and butter in a baking pan. Bake in 450-degree oven for 8 to 10 minutes. Add peanuts and butter to cooled mixture and beat until mixture loses gloss. Turn into a lightly greased 9 x 9 x 3-inch pan and cool. Cut in squares. 1 pound.

Mrs. Le Roy Butler, Atlanta, Georgia

BUTTER-RUM FUDGE

4 c. sugar	1 pt. marshmallow creme
1 lge. can evaporated milk	1 tsp. rum flavoring
1 c. butter or margarine	3/4 c. broken walnuts
2 6-oz. packages semisweet chocolate pieces	3/4 c. broken pecans

Mix the sugar, milk and butter in a saucepan and cook to soft-ball stage or to 236 degrees on candy thermometer, stirring frequently. Remove from heat and add chocolate pieces, marshmallow creme, rum flavoring, walnuts and pecans. Beat until chocolate is melted and well blended and pour into buttered 9 x 9 x 2-inch pan. Cool and cut in squares.

Mrs. Frank G. Scarborough, Norfolk, Virginia

PEPPERMINT-FLAVORED FUDGE

2 tbsp. butter	1 6-oz. package chocolate pieces
4 tsp. water	1/2 tsp. vanilla
1/2 tsp. salt	1/4 tsp. peppermint flavoring
3/4 lb. marshmallows	1 c. chopped walnuts

Place the butter in a saucepan and melt over low heat. Add the water, salt and marshmallows and heat, stirring frequently, until marshmallows are melted. Bring to a boil and cook for 1 to 2 minutes. Remove from heat. Add chocolate and stir until melted. Add the vanilla and peppermint flavorings and beat until thick. Add nuts and mix well. Pour into a greased pan and cool. Cut into squares.

Agnes Barnes, San Antonio, Texas

CHOCOLATE FUDGE

1 1/4 c. milk	2 tbsp. corn syrup
4 1-oz. squares unsweetened	1/4 c. butter
chocolate	1 tsp. vanilla
3 c. sugar	1 1/2 c. coarsely chopped nuts

Place the milk and chocolate in a heavy saucepan and place over low heat until chocolate melts. Add the sugar and corn syrup and stir until sugar dissolves. Wash sugar crystals from side of saucepan with damp cloth wrapped around a fork. Cook to soft-ball stage or 234 degrees on candy thermometer, stirring occasionally. Remove from heat. Add the butter and cool to lukewarm or 110 degrees without stirring. Add the vanilla and nuts and beat until mixture holds shape and begins to lose gloss. Pour onto greased platter or pan and cool until firm. Cut into squares and decorate with pecan halves, if desired. About 3 pounds.

CHRISTMAS BUTTER FUDGE

4 c. sugar	1 tsp. vanilla
2 c. milk	1/4 c. finely chopped candied
1/2 c. butter	cherries
1/4 tsp. salt	1/4 c. blanched pistachio nuts

Place the sugar, milk, butter and salt in a large saucepan and bring to boiling point, stirring constantly until sugar dissolves. Cook over moderate heat, stirring occasionally, until mixture forms a soft ball when dropped into cold water or 236 degrees on candy thermometer. Remove from heat immediately and place saucepan in cold water. Do not stir or beat until cooled to lukewarm. Add the vanilla and beat until thick and creamy. Add the cherries and nuts and mix quickly. Pour into greased 8-inch square pan and let stand at room temperature until firm. Cut into squares and decorate with whole cherries, if desired.

CHOCOLATE-SOUR CREAM FUDGE

3 c. sugar	6 tbsp. cocoa
1 c. sour cream	1/8 tsp. salt
1/8 tsp. soda	1 tsp. vanilla
4 tbsp. dark corn syrup	1 c. chopped nuts

Combine all ingredients except vanilla and nuts in a saucepan and bring to a boil. Reduce heat and cover. Cook for 3 minutes. Uncover and cook, stirring occasionally, until mixture reaches soft-ball stage. Let set until bottom of pan feels cool to the touch. Add vanilla and beat until mixture begins to lose gloss. Add the nuts and beat until thick. Pour into buttered pan and cut into squares.

Mrs. Carrie Horne, Macon, Georgia

HONEY FUDGE

2 c. sugar	1/4 c. honey
3/4 c. milk	2 tbsp. butter
1/4 c. cream	1 tsp. vanilla
1 sq. unsweetened chocolate	1 c. chopped nuts

Mix the sugar, milk, cream and chocolate in a saucepan and bring to a boil. Cook for 5 minutes. Add the honey and butter and cook to soft-ball stage. Cool and beat until thick. Add the vanilla and nuts and pour into a buttered pan. Cut into squares.

Theresa Brown, Charleston, South Carolina

MARSHMALLOW CREME FUDGE

4 1/2 c. sugar	12 oz. semisweet chocolate
Pinch of salt	pieces
1/2 c. butter	1 pt. marshmallow creme
1 tall can evaporated milk	2 c. chopped nuts
12 oz. German's sweet chocolate	

Combine the sugar, salt, butter and milk in a saucepan and bring to a boil. Cook for 6 minutes. Combine remaining ingredients in a large bowl. Add sugar mixture and beat until chocolate is melted and mixture is smooth. Pour into buttered pan and cool. Cut into squares.

Mrs. A. T. Gunter, Belden, Mississippi

CARAMEL CHOCOLATE FUDGE

2 c. (firmly packed) light	1/8 tsp. salt
brown sugar	1/2 c. light corn syrup
2 sq. chocolate	1/2 c. evaporated milk

1/2 c. milk	2 tbsp. butter
1 tsp. vanilla	2 c. chopped pecans

Blend the sugar, chocolate and salt in a saucepan. Stir in the corn syrup and milk and cook over medium heat, stirring, until mixture comes to a boil. Reduce heat and cook until mixture reaches the soft-ball stage, stirring occasionally. Remove from heat and cool for about 10 minutes. Add the vanilla, butter and pecans and beat until mixture loses gloss. Pour into a buttered square pan and cut in squares.

Mrs. Florine M. Suire, Erath, Louisiana

CHERRY CREME FUDGE

4 c. sugar	2 tsp. vanilla
1 c. half and half	1/2 c. marshmallow creme
1 c. butter	1 c. pecan halves
1/2 c. light corn syrup	1/2 c. coarsely chopped candied
1/2 tsp. salt	cherries

Combine the sugar, half and half, butter, corn syrup and salt in a heavy 4-quart saucepan. Bring to a boil over moderate heat, stirring constantly until sugar is dissolved. Reduce heat to low and cook, stirring occasionally, until mixture reaches soft-ball stage. Remove from heat. Place saucepan in cold water and cool to lukewarm. Add vanilla and marshmallow creme and beat until mixture loses shine. Add pecans and cherries and beat until thick. Pour into well-greased 9-inch square pan and cool until firm. Cut into squares. Decorate top of each square with a pecan or cherry half, if desired.

SIMPLE CHOCOLATE FUDGE

2 c. sugar	1 stick butter
1/4 c. cocoa	1 tsp. vanilla
1/4 c. milk	1 c. chopped nuts (opt.)
1/8 tsp. salt	

Mix the sugar, cocoa, milk, salt and butter in a saucepan and bring to a boil. Cook for 3 minutes. Add vanilla and nuts and beat until creamy. Pour into a greased pan and cool. Cut into squares.

Mrs. Joe Edwards, Houston, Mississippi

BUTTERMILK FUDGE

2 c. sugar	1 tsp. soda
2 tbsp. light corn syrup	Pinch of salt
1 c. buttermilk	1 tsp. vanilla
2 tbsp. butter	1 c. chopped nuts

Combine all ingredients except vanilla and nuts in a deep, heavy saucepan and bring to a boil. Cook, stirring constantly, until small amount of mixture forms a soft ball in cold water. Remove from heat and add vanilla. Beat until creamy. Add the nuts and stir until mixed. Pour into a greased pan and cool. Cut into squares.

Mrs. Lovic Langheld, Minden, Louisiana

BUTTERSCOTCH PUDDING FUDGE

1 pkg. butterscotch pudding	1 1/2 c. chopped pecans
1/2 c. (packed) brown sugar	1 tbsp. butter
1/2 c. evaporated milk	1 tsp. vanilla
1 c. sugar	

Combine first 4 ingredients in a saucepan and bring to a boil. Cook for 5 minutes, stirring constantly. Remove from heat and add remaining ingredients. Beat until cool. Pour into a buttered dish and cut into squares.

Mrs. Evelyn Waring, Jackson, Tennessee

MEXICAN FUDGE

1 c. milk	1 c. chopped pecans
3 c. sugar	1 tsp. vanilla

Mix the milk and 2 cups sugar in a saucepan and cook for 15 minutes. Melt remaining sugar in an iron skillet over low heat, stirring constantly, and add to the milk mixture. Add the pecans and vanilla and beat until thick. Pour onto well-buttered pan and cool. Cut into squares.

Mrs. Valla Killian, Acme, Louisiana

PINEAPPLE FUDGE

1 c. evaporated milk
3 c. sugar
2 tbsp. butter or margarine

1 c. drained crushed pineapple
2 tsp. lemon juice

Combine the milk, sugar and butter in a saucepan and bring to boiling point. Add the pineapple and cook over medium heat to soft-ball stage or 235 degrees on a candy thermometer, stirring constantly. Cool. Add the lemon juice and beat until thick. Turn into a buttered pan and cut in squares. Decorate with pecan halves, if desired.

Louise Bollinger, Sweetwater, Texas

SOUR CREAM BUTTERSCOTCH FUDGE

1/4 c. butter or margarine
1 c. (packed) brown sugar
1 c. sugar

3/4 c. sour cream
1 tsp. vanilla
1/2 c. chopped nuts

Melt the butter in a heavy saucepan. Stir in the sugars and sour cream and cook, stirring, to soft-ball stage. Cool to room temperature without stirring. Beat until thickened. Stir in the vanilla and nuts and spread in a greased pan. Cool and cut into squares.

Mrs. W. A. Dobbs, Baltimore, Maryland

SOUR CREAM-WALNUT FUDGE

2 c. sugar
2.tbsp. light corn syrup
2 tbsp. butter
3/4 c. sour cream

1 tsp. vanilla
1/2 c. chopped black
   walnuts

Mix the sugar, corn syrup, butter and sour cream in a saucepan and cook over medium heat until mixture reaches the soft-ball stage. Cool slightly. Add the vanilla and walnuts and cool to room temperature. Beat until thick and pour into a buttered platter. Cut into squares.

Mrs. James L. Patton, Lexington, Kentucky

VANILLA FUDGE

1 1/2 lb. sugar
1/2 c. light corn syrup
1 1/4 c. evaporated milk

1/4 lb. margarine or butter
1 tsp. vanilla

Combine the sugar, corn syrup, milk and margarine in a saucepan and cook over medium heat to a firm-ball stage. Remove from heat. Add the vanilla and beat until mixture loses glossy appearance. Place in greased plates and cool. Cut in squares. 2 pounds.

Elizabeth Triplett, Stange Creek, West Virginia

129

CHOCOLATE-COVERED CHERRIES

1 lb. bitter chocolate	1/3 c. (about) evaporated
1/2 oz. paraffin	milk
1 1-lb. box confectioners'	1 lge. jar maraschino cherries
sugar	with stems, drained
1 tsp. vanilla	

Melt the chocolate and paraffin in a double boiler and cool slightly. Mix the confectioners' sugar, vanilla and enough milk for thick consistency. Remove a small amount of sugar mixture and flatten to the size of a half dollar. Wrap around a cherry, leaving only stem uncovered. Hold by stem and dip into chocolate mixture. Place on waxed paper. Repeat with remaining sugar mixture and cherries and let set for 2 hours.

Mrs. Mary W. Whitehead, Nashville, Tennessee

CHOCOLATE-COVERED CHERRIES AND NUTS

4 tbsp. butter	1 tsp. vanilla
1 1-lb. box powdered sugar	1 bottle cherries, drained
4 tbsp. sweetened condensed	1/2 c. chopped nuts
milk	1 1-lb. package chocolate
Pinch of salt	1/4 cake paraffin

Cream the butter and sugar in a bowl and stir in the milk, small amount at a time. Add salt and vanilla. Roll the cherries in sugar mixture to coat each cherry well. Add the nuts to remaining sugar mixture and shape in oblong rolls. Melt chocolate and paraffin in top of a double boiler over boiling water. Dip cherries and nut rolls, one at a time, in chocolate mixture and place on waxed paper to cool.

Mrs. Frances E. Poole, Forsyth, Georgia

CHOCOLATE-COVERED COCONUT

1 c. sugar	1/2 tsp. vanilla
1 1/2 c. light corn syrup	1 lb. sweet chocolate
1/2 c. water	1/2 cake paraffin
4 c. shredded coconut	

Combine the sugar, corn syrup and water in a heavy saucepan and cook over low heat, stirring constantly, until sugar is dissolved. Cook to the soft-ball stage or 236 degrees on a candy thermometer, wiping off sugar crystals on side of saucepan while cooking. Remove from heat and add the coconut and vanilla. Pour onto a marble or plastic counter top and cool. Shape into a ball and cover with plastic wrap. Place in refrigerator until chilled. Melt the chocolate and paraffin in a double boiler. Shape the coconut mixture into balls and dip in chocolate. Place on waxed paper to cool. 2 pounds.

Mrs. Walter Jones, Houston, Texas

CHOCOLATE STRAWBERRIES

1 6-oz. package semisweet   **1 pt. fresh strawberries**
   chocolate pieces

Melt chocolate over hot, not boiling, water. Remove from heat. Wash and drain the strawberries. Hold strawberries by stem ends and dip into chocolate to coat. Place on waxed paper and let stand at room temperature until chocolate is set. Place chocolate over hot water until dipping consistency if too thick before all strawberries are coated.

SNOWCAP STRAWBERRIES

2 pt. fresh strawberries   **1 1/2 tsp. white corn syrup**
1 egg white   **1/4 tsp. salt**
3/4 c. sugar   **1/2 tsp. vanilla**
1/4 c. water

Wash and drain the strawberries. Combine the egg white, sugar, water, syrup and salt in top of a double boiler and blend with electric mixer. Place over rapidly boiling water and beat at high speed until mixture forms peaks when beater is raised. Remove from heat and add vanilla. Beat until thick and of spreading consistency. Remove from water. Hold strawberries by stem ends and dip into vanilla mixture to coat. Place on waxed paper and let stand at room temperature until coating is set.

CHOCOLATE-COVERED DATES

2 sticks butter	Evaporated milk
2 1-lb. boxes confectioners'	Pitted dates
sugar	8 sq. unsweetened chocolate
2 tsp. vanilla	1/2 block paraffin

Cream the butter in a bowl. Sift the sugar and add to butter gradually. Knead on a flat surface until very stiff. Add vanilla and mix. Add milk, small amount at a time, until mixture is thick and smooth. Shape the fondant around dates and refrigerate for 20 to 30 minutes. Melt the chocolate and paraffin in a double boiler and cool slightly. Dip fondant-covered dates in chocolate and place on waxed paper to cool.

Pat Roberts, Durham, North Carolina

DIPPED DREAM CREAMS

1 c. light cream	1/2 tsp. vanilla
2 c. sugar	1/4 c. chopped nuts
1 tbsp. light corn syrup	1 lb. semisweet chocolate
1/8 tsp. salt	1/2 cake paraffin

Scald the cream. Combine the sugar, 1/2 cup cream and corn syrup in a heavy saucepan. Place over medium heat and stir constantly until mixture comes to a boil. Cook, stirring occasionally, to soft-ball stage or 238 degrees on a candy thermometer. Add remaining cream slowly, stirring constantly, and cook to soft-ball stage again. Remove from heat. Pour onto a marble counter or chilled baking pan. Let stand for 5 minutes. Cut several light gashes with a knife but do not cut through to the counter or pan. Add the salt and vanilla. Work with a wide spatula, turning the outside edge over the center, until mixture is thick and firm. Knead with hands until creamy and fold in the nuts while kneading. Place in a container and cover tightly. Store in refrigerator until chilled. Shape in balls. Melt the chocolate and paraffin in a double boiler and cool slightly. Dip the balls in chocolate and place on waxed paper to cool.

Mrs. Sarah Jones, Palm Beach, Florida

OKLAHOMA CHERRY DIVINITY

2 c. sugar	2 egg whites, stiffly beaten
1/2 c. light corn syrup	1 tsp. vanilla
1/4 tsp. salt	3/4 c. chopped candied
1/2 c. water	cherries

Mix the sugar, syrup, salt and water in a saucepan and place over low heat, stirring, until sugar is dissolved. Cook, without stirring, to hard-ball stage or 248 degrees on candy thermometer, wiping off sugar crystals with a damp cloth during cooking. Remove from heat and pour into egg whites gradually, beating constantly. Add vanilla and beat until mixture will hold shape when dropped from a spoon. Add the cherries and drop by spoonfuls onto waxed paper.

Muriel Liles, Sterling, Oklahoma

CAN'T FAIL DIVINITY

2 c. sugar	1 pt. marshmallow creme
1/2 c. water	1/2 c. chopped nuts or fruit
Pinch of salt	1 tsp. vanilla

Mix the sugar, water and salt in a saucepan and cook until small amount of mixture forms a hard ball in cold water. Place the marshmallow creme in a mixing bowl and beat in hot syrup slowly. Continue beating until thick. Fold in the nuts and vanilla and drop from spoon onto waxed paper.

Mrs. E. G. Roberson, Jr., DeWitt, Arkansas

PERFECT DIVINITY

5 c. sugar	2 lge. egg whites
1 c. light corn syrup	1 tsp. vanilla
1 c. water	2 c. chopped nuts
1/4 tsp. salt	

Combine the sugar, syrup, water and salt in a saucepan and stir until sugar dissolves. Heat to boiling point and cover. Boil for 2 minutes. Uncover and cook to soft-ball stage or to 238 degrees on candy thermometer. Beat the egg whites until stiff but not dry. Pour syrup over egg whites slowly, beating constantly with electric mixer, then beat until candy is cool and holds shape. Stir in the vanilla and nuts and drop from teaspoon onto waxed paper.

Mrs. Verna K. Arrington, Sweeny, Texas

PASTEL DIVINITY

3 c. sugar	1 3-oz. package flavored gelatin
3/4 c. light corn syrup	1 c. chopped nuts
3/4 c. water	1/2 c. grated coconut
2 egg whites	1 tsp. vanilla

Mix the sugar, syrup and water in a saucepan and stir until sugar is dissolved. Cook to hard-ball stage. Beat egg whites until foamy. Add the gelatin gradually and beat until stiff. Pour syrup into egg white mixture slowly, beating constantly, then beat until candy holds shape and loses gloss. Fold in the nuts, coconut and vanilla. Drop from a spoon onto waxed paper and cool.

Betty Fuller, Memphis, Tennessee

LOUISIANA CREAM PRALINES

1 1-lb. box light brown sugar	1 tbsp. butter
1/8 tsp. salt	2 c. pecan halves
3/4 c. evaporated milk	

Mix the brown sugar, salt, evaporated milk and butter in a 2-quart saucepan. Cook and stir over low heat until sugar is dissolved. Add pecans and cook over medium heat to soft-ball stage or to 234 degrees on candy thermometer, stirring constantly. Remove from heat and cool for 5 minutes. Stir rapidly until mixture is thickened. Drop rapidly from a tablespoon onto aluminum foil or a lightly greased baking sheet to form patties. Stir in several drops of hot water if candy becomes too stiff to handle easily. Let stand until cool and set. About 20 pralines.

RASPBERRY DIVINITY

3 c. sugar	1 3-oz. package raspberry
3/4 c. light corn syrup	gelatin
1/2 c. hot water	1 c. chopped nuts
2 egg whites	

Mix the sugar, syrup and water in a saucepan and cook to hard-ball stage or 252 degrees on candy thermometer, stirring frequently. Beat the egg whites until foamy. Add the gelatin slowly and beat until stiff. Beat in the hot syrup mixture slowly and continue beating until mixture will hold shape. Add the nuts and drop from teaspoon onto waxed paper.

Maude Dixon, Bentonville, Arkansas

CHOCOLATE-WALNUT PUFFS

1 c. semisweet chocolate pieces	1/2 c. sugar
2 egg whites	1/2 tsp. vanilla
1/8 tsp. salt	1/2 tsp. vinegar
	3/4 c. chopped walnuts

Melt the chocolate pieces over warm water. Beat the egg whites with salt in a bowl until foamy. Add sugar gradually and beat until stiff peaks form. Beat in the vanilla and vinegar and fold in chocolate and walnuts. Drop from a teaspoon onto a greased cookie sheet. Bake at 350 degrees for 10 minutes. 3 dozen.

Mrs. Thomas Leonard, Mobile, Alabama

SEAFOAM NUT KISSES

1 egg white	1/8 tsp. salt
1/4 c. instant nonfat dry milk	1 tbsp. flour
1 tbsp. water	1 c. chopped nuts
3/4 c. (packed) brown sugar	

Beat the egg white, dry milk and water in a small mixer bowl with electric mixer at high speed until stiff. Beat in the brown sugar, 1 tablespoon at a time, then beat until thick, scraping sides of bowl frequently. Mix the salt, flour and nuts and fold into egg white mixture. Drop by teaspoonfuls onto greased and floured cookie sheet. Bake in 325-degree oven for about 15 minutes or until light brown. Remove from cookie sheet and cool on wire rack. 2 dozen.

Mrs. Ann Rushing, Pachuta, Mississippi

BROWNIE NUGGETS

2 tbsp. cocoa	1/2 stick margarine
1/4 c. milk	1 c. quick-cooking oats
1 c. sugar	1/4 c. peanut butter

Place the cocoa in a saucepan and add milk gradually, stirring constantly. Stir in the sugar and margarine and bring to a boil. Cook for 1 minute. Remove from heat and stir in the oats and peanut butter. Drop by teaspoonfuls onto waxed paper and let stand until firm.

Mrs. C. J. Harris, Rockmart, Georgia

PARTY PUFFS

4 egg whites	1 tsp. vanilla
1 1/2 c. sugar	1 1/2 c. chopped pecans

Beat the egg whites and sugar in top of a double boiler over hot water until warm. Remove from water and beat until firm peaks form. Fold in the vanilla and pecans. Drop by teaspoonfuls on an ungreased cookie sheet. Bake at 325 degrees for 12 to 15 minutes. 5 dozen.

Amy Cottingham, Annapolis, Maryland

CHOCOLATE ENCHANTMENTS

1   14-oz. package caramels
3 tbsp. water
1/2 c. semisweet chocolate pieces

3/4 c. chopped nutmeats
1 c. quick rolled oats

Place the caramels and water in top of a double boiler over boiling water. Heat, stirring occasionally, until caramels are melted. Reduce heat until water in double boiler is hot, not boiling. Add chocolate pieces and stir until melted. Remove from heat and stir in nutmeats and oats. Drop quickly by teaspoonfuls onto waxed paper. Chill. 3 dozen.

CHOCOLATE DELIGHTS

2 c. sugar
4 tbsp. cocoa
1 c. cream
24 marshmallows

2 c. graham cracker crumbs
1 c. chopped nuts
2 tsp. vanilla

Mix the sugar, cocoa and cream in a saucepan and cook to soft-ball stage, stirring constantly. Cool slightly, then add the marshmallows, crumbs, nuts and vanilla. Mix well. Drop by teaspoonfuls on waxed paper.

Mrs. Wallace Howard, Selman, Oklahoma

WALNUT MERINGUE KISSES

2 egg whites
4 dashes of salt

1/2 c. sugar
2 tsp. cinnamon

1/4 tsp. cloves   1 c. chopped black walnuts
1/4 tsp. nutmeg   Pecan halves

Beat egg whites in a bowl until stiff, adding salt and sugar gradually. Fold in the spices and walnuts. Drop by spoonfuls onto greased baking sheet and place a pecan half on each cookie. Bake at 250 degrees for 35 to 40 minutes. 4 dozen.

Mrs. George A. Zirkle, Jr., Knoxville, Tennessee

CHOCOLATE-PEANUT CANDY

2 c. sugar   1/2 c. milk
3 tbsp. cocoa   1/2 c. peanut butter
1/2 tsp. salt   4 1/2 c. oats
1 stick margarine   1 tsp. vanilla

Mix the sugar, cocoa, salt, margarine and milk in a saucepan and bring to a boil. Cook for 2 minutes and remove from heat. Add the peanut butter, oats and vanilla and mix thoroughly. Drop from teaspoon on waxed paper and cool.

Amelia Terrebonne, Loranger, Louisiana

MINTS

3 c. sugar   Pinch of cream of tartar
1 c. light corn syrup   Oil of peppermint to taste
2 c. hot water   Food coloring

Mix the sugar, corn syrup and hot water in a saucepan and cook to soft-ball stage. Pour into a bowl. Add the cream of tartar and let stand for 10 minutes. Beat until thick. Add the oil of peppermint and desired amount of food coloring and mix well. Drop by teaspoonfuls onto waxed paper.

Mrs. G. L. Waters, Knoxville, Tennessee

PEDRO'S MEXICAN CANDY

2 c. sugar   1/2 tsp. vanilla
3/4 c. milk   1/2 c. broken pecans
1/2 tsp. soda   Salt
2 tbsp. butter

Mix the sugar, milk and soda in a large saucepan and cook until small amount of mixture forms a soft ball in cold water. Remove from heat. Add the butter, vanilla and pecans and beat until creamy. Drop from spoon onto waxed paper sprinkled with salt. The salt on waxed paper is the secret of the candy.

Mrs. R. W. Harper, Harlingen, Texas

fruit candies & nut confections

Dried and fresh fruits and all types of nuts form the basis of many delicious candies. *Southern Living* homemakers have used the fruits and nuts available in their verdant region to create mouth-watering candies – like the world-famous pralines.

This candy originated with the Creoles who settled in and around New Orleans. They adapted it from a recipe brought with them from Europe. When they couldn't find the black walnuts the recipe specified, they substituted pecans – and pralines were born! That's the kind of inventiveness that typifies southern cooking – and it is demonstrated in the recipes that follow.

You'll find several recipes for pralines, of course. But you'll also find recipes for Mocha Peanut Clusters, a candy with a wonderful blend of chocolate and coffee highlighted with peanut-y flavor.

Fruits and nuts from other regions are similarly transformed into sugary delights, in such candies as Swedish Nuts, Candied Holiday Nuts, Apricot Bells, and Date Fingers. And these are just some of the recipes you'll enjoy.

For candies that are chewy and scrumptious as well as nourishing, choose from the recipes you'll find in the pages that follow. These are time-tested favorites just waiting to bring you the warm compliments of your satisfied friends and family members.

CHOCOLATE-APPLE ROLLIES

1 12-oz. package semisweet chocolate chips	2/3 c. drained chopped maraschino cherries
1 c. canned applesauce	1 c. chopped walnuts
1 tsp. almond extract	1 3 1/2-oz. can flaked coconut
5 c. confectioners' sugar	

Combine the chocolate chips, applesauce and almond extract in a heavy aluminum saucepan and stir over low heat until chocolate is melted and ingredients are blended. Stir in the sugar, cherries and walnuts and chill for about 1 hour or until firm. Shape into 1 1/2-inch balls and roll in coconut. About 5 dozen.

APPLE CANDY

4 env. unflavored gelatin	1 tsp. vanilla
4 c. sugar	1 c. chopped nuts
2 1/2 c. applesauce	Powdered sugar

Combine the gelatin and the sugar and stir into the applesauce. Cook for 15 minutes, stirring frequently. Add the vanilla and nuts and then pour into a buttered pan. Chill until firm. Cut and roll in powdered sugar. 4 dozen.

Mrs. Roberta Horan, Wichita Falls, Texas

APRICOT-MARSHMALLOW DREAMS

1 1/2 c. dried apricots	1/4 can sweetened condensed milk
1 c. shredded coconut	Sugar
1/4 lb. marshmallows	

Grind the apricots, coconut and marshmallows together and add the milk. Mix well. Shape into small balls and roll in the sugar. Let stand for 30 minutes, then roll in sugar again.

Mrs. Henry Gibson, Mobile, Alabama

APRICOT BALLS

1 1/2 c. ground dried apricots	2/3 c. sweetened condensed milk
2 c. shredded coconut	Confectioners' sugar

Combine the apricots and coconut. Add the milk and mix well. Shape into small balls and roll in confectioners' sugar. Let stand until firm.

Mrs. Lee McCallister, Palestine, Texas

EASY APRICOT CANDY

1 10-oz. package dried	1 orange
apricots	1 c. sugar

Grind the apricots and orange in a food chopper and add the sugar. Cook in a double boiler until thick. Drop from tablespoon into sugar and roll until coated. Cool on waxed paper until firm. 30 servings.

Mrs. Warren Lee, Atlanta, Georgia

CHERRY-RUM BALLS

1 c. vanilla wafer crumbs	2 tbsp. light corn syrup
1 c. powdered sugar	1/4 c. rum
1 1/2 c. chopped pecans	1/2 c. sugar
2 tbsp. cocoa	Red candied cherry halves

Combine the crumbs, powdered sugar, 1 cup pecans and cocoa and mix. Add the syrup and rum and stir until well combined. Shape into 1-inch balls and roll half of the balls in sugar and half in remaining pecans. Moisten cut sides of cherry halves with additional corn syrup and press 1 on each sugar-coated rum ball. Store in airtight container. One-fourth cup cream and 1 teaspoon rum extract may be substituted for the rum. 3 dozen.

Mrs. Jerome Vale, Hyattsville, Maryland

COATED COCONUT CANDY

1 stick butter, melted	1 can sweetened condensed milk
2 boxes confectioners' sugar	1 box semisweet chocolate
2 boxes flaked coconut	1/2 block paraffin
1 tbsp. vanilla	

Combine the butter, sugar, coconut, vanilla and milk and mix well. Shape into balls. Chill for 1 hour. Melt the chocolate and paraffin in top of double boiler. Dip balls into chocolate mixture, then place on waxed paper to harden. 4 pounds.

Mrs. Georgina Hubbard, Guston, Kentucky

CRANBERRY CRYSTALS

1 egg white	**1 c. fresh cranberries**
1/2 tsp. water	**1 c. sugar**

Beat the egg white and water lightly in a bowl until blended. Dip cranberries in egg white mixture until completely coated, then roll in sugar. Place on waxed paper and let stand at room temperature until dry.

DATE FINGERS

1 c. sugar	**1 tsp. vanilla**
1 stick margarine	**1 c. chopped nuts**
1 c. chopped dates	**2 c. rice cereal**
1 egg, beaten	**Coconut**

Combine the sugar and margarine and stir until melted over low heat. Add the dates, then the egg and stir until blended. Cook over low heat until mixture comes to a boil, then cook for 10 minutes, stirring constantly. Remove from heat and add the vanilla, nuts and cereal, then cool. Roll into finger-sized pieces and roll in coconut.

Mrs. Ralph Phillips, Honea Path, South Carolina

CANDY FRUIT ROLL

1 c. chopped dates	**1/2 c. white raisins**
1 c. chopped dried figs	**1/2 c. sugar**
1/2 c. chopped pecans	**1/2 c. light corn syrup**
1/2 c. shredded coconut	**1/2 c. milk**

Combine the dates, figs, pecans, coconut and raisins in a large mixing bowl. Combine the sugar, syrup and milk and cook over medium heat to soft-ball stage. Remove from heat and beat for 2 minutes. Pour over fruit mixture and stir until blended. Cool and shape into rolls, 6 inches long and 2 1/2 inches wide. Cool completely before slicing. 15 servings.

Mrs. Constance Terry, Ocala, Florida

ORANGE-APRICOT BALLS

1 orange	1 c. chopped nuts
1 pkg. dried apricots	Shredded coconut
1 1/2 c. sugar	

Remove the seed and membrane from the orange and grind with apricots in food chopper, using fine blade. Add the sugar and place in a heavy boiler or frying pan. Simmer until clear, then add the nuts. Cool. Form into small balls and roll in coconut.

Mrs. Hall Ouzts, Callison, South Carolina

CHERRY-DATE ROLL

2 c. evaporated milk	1/4 lb. candied cherries,
4 c. sugar	chopped
1/4 lb. butter or margarine	1 lb. pecans, chopped
1 lb. pitted dates, chopped	Powdered sugar

Combine the milk and sugar and cook until thickened. Add butter, and cook, stirring constantly, to soft-ball stage. Add the dates and cook until thick. Remove from heat and add cherries and pecans. Beat until hardened. Pour on a damp cloth and roll into a long roll. Let stand until hard. Roll in powdered sugar. 5-6 pounds.

Mrs. Charles Bowman, Lincoln, Kentucky

CHRISTMAS CHEER CANDY

3 c. sugar	1/2 lb. candied pineapple,
1 c. light corn syrup	chopped
1 1/2 c. light cream	1/2 lb. walnuts, chopped
1 tsp. vanilla	1/2 lb. Brazil nuts, chopped
1/2 lb. candied cherries, chopped	1/2 lb. pecans, chopped

Combine the sugar, syrup and cream in a heavy saucepan and bring to a boil. Boil for 8 minutes, stirring constantly or until mixture forms a soft ball in water. Remove from heat and add the vanilla. Beat until mixture begins to thicken or is light in color. Stir in the fruits and nuts. Pour into a 10 x 15-inch buttered pan. Cool and cut into squares. Candy improves with age and will keep for several weeks. May also be frozen if desired. 5 pounds.

Mrs. Faye Hubbard, Tuscaloosa, Alabama

MEXICAN ORANGE CANDY

3 c. sugar
1 1/2 c. milk, scalded
1 c. chopped walnuts

Grated rind of 2 oranges
1/2 c. butter

Place 1 cup sugar in a skillet and cook over low heat, stirring constantly until dissolved. Add milk and remaining sugar and bring to a boil. Cook to hard-ball stage. Add walnuts, rind and butter and beat until creamy. Drop on waxed paper and cool.

Mrs. Bessie Walls, Pawnee, Oklahoma

GOLDEN STICKS

1 12-oz. package dried apricots
1 c. golden raisins

1 can flaked coconut
1 can sweetened condensed milk
1 can finely chopped coconut

Force the apricots and raisins through the medium blade of food chopper twice. Add the flaked coconut and milk and mix well. Wet hands and shape mixture into sticks about 1 1/2 x 1/2 inch. Roll in chopped coconut and let stand for about 20 minutes before placing in airtight container. Refrigerate or freeze. 60 pieces.

Mrs. Homer Davis, Leesburg, Florida

CHERRY-COCONUT TRUFFLES

4 1-oz. squares chocolate
2 tbsp. butter
2 tbsp. evaporated milk
1 c. confectioners' sugar

5 oz. candied cherries with stems
1/2 c. flaked coconut

Break the chocolate into squares and place in a bowl with the butter and milk. Place over boiling water and stir until chocolate and butter are melted. Remove from water. Sift the sugar into chocolate mixture and mix well. Refrigerate until chilled. Shape 1 teaspoon chocolate mixture around each cherry, leaving small part of stem end of the cherries showing. Roll balls in the coconut, leaving the tops of the cherries uncovered.

ORANGE CARAMELS

1 1-lb. box powdered sugar
2 tsp. lemon juice
1/2 c. butter

1/2 c. milk
Juice and grated rind of 1 orange

Mix all ingredients except orange rind in a saucepan and place over low heat, stirring, until sugar is dissolved. Bring to a boil and cook to soft-ball stage or to 240 degrees on a candy thermometer. Remove from heat and pour into a bowl. Stir in the orange rind and beat until very thick. Pour into a greased 8-inch square pan and chill for about 2 hours or until firm. Cut into 1-inch squares.

RASPBERRY PASTILLES

1 box frozen raspberries
1 1/2 c. powdered sugar

4 env. unflavored gelatin

Wash the raspberries in a sieve under hot, running water and drain well. Place in a saucepan with 2 tablespoons water and cook until soft. Add 1 1/3 cups sugar and cook over low heat, stirring, until sugar is dissolved. Bring to a boil and cook for 5 minutes. Remove from heat and press through a fine sieve into a large bowl. Soften the gelatin in 2 tablespoons water. Add to the raspberry mixture and stir until dissolved. Pour into a greased 8-inch square pan and refrigerate for about 4 hours or until firm. Turn out onto a greased surface and cut into diamond shapes. Toss in remaining sugar.

FROSTED GRAPES

1/2 lb. black grapes
1/2 lb. white grapes

1/2 c. powdered sugar
1 egg white

Wash the grapes and break into pairs, keeping the stalks attached. Dry the grapes carefully with a clean, soft cloth. Place the sugar in a small plate. Place the egg white in a bowl. Dip each pair of grapes into the egg white, then coat very thickly with sugar. Shake off excess sugar and place on waxed paper. Let set for 24 hours to dry.

MERINGUE CANDY

2 egg whites	1/2 c. chopped dates
2 c. light brown sugar	1/2 c. diced candied cherries
2 c. sliced Brazil nuts	and pineapple

Beat the egg whites until stiff, then beat in the brown sugar gradually. Stir in the nuts, dates, and candied fruit. Drop from a teaspoon onto a greased baking sheet. Bake at 250 degrees for 30 minutes. Remove from baking sheet immediately and cool. 5 dozen candies.

Josie Ray Bloom, Charleston, South Carolina

MERRY FRUIT CONFECTION

1 c. chopped dried figs	1/2 c. sugar
1 c. raisins	1 tsp. vanilla
1 c. pitted dates	Shredded coconut
1 c. nuts	

Force the figs, raisins, dates and nuts through food chopper. Add the sugar and vanilla and knead well. Press into a square cake pan. Let stand in a cool place overnight. Cut into squares and sprinkle with coconut. 20 servings.

Mrs. Maggie Murfey, Covington, Kentucky

POPCORN-FRUIT BARS

1 c. sugar	2 qt. popcorn
1/2 c. water	1 c. small colored gumdrops
1 c. white corn syrup	1 c. chopped pecans
2 tbsp. margarine	1/2 c. chopped candied pineapple
Food coloring (opt.)	1/2 c. chopped candied cherries

Combine the first 4 ingredients and cook over medium heat, stirring constantly until sugar is dissolved. Cook to soft-ball stage. Add several drops of food coloring. Combine remaining ingredients and pour the syrup over mixture. Mix until well coated. Press into slightly greased oblong cake pan. Cool until firm and cut into bars for serving.

Mrs. George Okey, Dimmitt, Texas

ORANGE PEEL WITH COCONUT

2 lge. oranges	Flaked coconut
Sugar	

Wash the oranges and remove the peel in quarters. Scrape off excess white inner skin and cut peel into strips. Place in saucepan and cover with water. Bring to a boil, then drain off water. Repeat process 2 more times. Measure peel and combine in saucepan with an equal amount of sugar. Cover with water. Bring to a boil and cook until syrup is almost absorbed. Remove from heat and drain on racks for 1 minute. Roll quickly in coconut. 1 pound.

Adelaide Newsley, Tampa, Florida

PAPAYA CANDY

1 lge. green papaya	**1 c. sugar**
1 tsp. soda	**1 stick cinnamon**

Peel papaya and cut into strips about 1/8 inch thick. Soak in water to cover with soda overnight, then drain. Cover with water and cook for 10 minutes. Drain. Combine 1 cup water, sugar and cinnamon and bring to a boil, stirring to dissolve sugar. Add the papaya and cook slowly for 1 hour. Cool and serve with a sharp cheese. 12 servings.

Mrs. F. L. Quinones, Homestead, Florida

PINK AND WHITE CANDIES

3/4 c. butter or margarine	**2 tsp. maraschino cherry juice**
2 c. confectioners' sugar	**2 tbsp. finely chopped**
2 tsp. lemon juice	**maraschino cherries**
1/2 tsp. grated lemon peel	**3 drops of red food coloring**
2 c. quick or old-fashioned	**2/3 c. flaked or shredded**
oats	**coconut**

Cream the butter in a bowl. Add the sugar gradually and beat until well blended. Divide mixture in half. Add the lemon juice, lemon peel and 1 cup oats to half the mixture and mix. Add the cherry juice, cherries, food coloring and remaining oats to remaining half and mix. Chill both mixtures for 2 to 3 hours. Shape the lemon mixture into 18 balls and the cherry mixture into 18 balls. Roll in the coconut and refrigerate until chilled. 3 dozen.

CREAMY THREE-NUT CANDY

3 c. sugar	2 c. chopped pecans
2 c. light cream	2 c. chopped walnuts
1 c. light corn syrup	2 c. chopped Brazil nuts

Combine all ingredients and cook over low heat to 238 degrees on candy thermometer or to soft-ball stage. Remove from heat and stir until creamy and thickened. Turn into a large greased baking dish and pack down with a spoon. Cool thoroughly and remove from pan. Wrap in foil. Slice paper thin to serve. 4 1/2 pounds.

Mrs. Elaine Mixby, Pensacola, Florida

FILBERT DELIGHTS

2 egg whites	1 tsp. vanilla
2/3 c. sugar	1 1/2 c. ground filberts
1/4 tsp. salt	

Beat the egg whites until stiff, adding sugar gradually. Fold in salt, vanilla and filberts. Drop from teaspoon onto slightly oiled cookie sheet. Bake until lightly browned at 300 degrees for 10 to 12 minutes. 3 to 4 dozen.

Emma Walker, Lubbock, Texas

FILBERT CONFECTION CREAMS

1 c. chopped filberts	1/4 tsp. salt
1/2 c. butter	1 egg
1/4 c. sugar	1 3/4 c. vanilla wafer crumbs
2 tbsp. cocoa	1/2 c. flaked coconut
2 tsp. vanilla	

Spread the filberts in a shallow baking pan. Bake in 350-degree oven for 5 to 10 minutes, stirring occasionally, until lightly browned. Combine the butter, sugar, cocoa, vanilla, salt and egg in a saucepan and cook over low heat until thickened and glossy. Add the crumbs, filberts and coconut and mix well. Press into a 9-inch square pan.

Icing

1/3 c. butter	2 c. sifted confectioners' sugar
1 egg	4 sq. semisweet chocolate
1/2 tsp. peppermint extract	

Cream the butter in a bowl. Add egg and extract and beat well. Beat in sugar until smooth and creamy. Spread over filbert mixture and chill until firm. Melt the chocolate over hot water and spread over Icing. Cool until chocolate is partially set, then cut into 1 1/4 x 3/4-inch bars. Refrigerate until ready to serve.

Photograph for this recipe on page 138.

CHOCOLATE-PECAN DIPS

1 6-oz. package semisweet
  chocolate pieces

Pecan halves

Heat the chocolate pieces over boiling water until melted, stirring frequently. Remove from water and cool until partially thickened. Place 1 teaspoon chocolate between 2 pecan halves and cool completely on waxed paper.

FUDGE-NUT BALLS

1 6-oz. package semisweet
  chocolate pieces
3 tbsp. corn syrup
1/2 c. evaporated milk
1 tsp. vanilla

1/2 c. powdered sugar
1 c. finely chopped unsalted
  nuts
2 1/2 c. vanilla wafer crumbs

Heat the chocolate pieces in a 2-quart bowl over boiling water until melted. Remove bowl from water and stir in the corn syrup, milk and vanilla gradually. Add the sugar and mix until smooth. Stir in the nuts. Fold in the wafer crumbs, about 1/4 at a time, and mix well. Let stand at room temperature for 30 minutes. Shape into 1-inch balls and roll balls, one at a time, in additional powdered sugar. Chill. About 4 1/2 dozen.

SWEDISH NUTS

2 egg whites	1 1/2 c. pecan halves
1 c. sugar	1 c. walnut halves
1/4 tsp. salt	1 c. almonds
1/2 c. butter, melted	

Beat the egg whites with the sugar and salt until stiff. Place the butter and nuts in a baking pan, then fold in meringue. Bake at 325 degrees for about 30 minutes, stirring every 10 minutes. Cool and remove from pan.

Mrs. Hazel Hampton, Hickory, North Carolina

ALMOND-STUFFED DATES

1 box dates	Grated rind of 1 orange
1/4 c. ground almonds	Orange food coloring
2/3 c. powdered sugar	1 egg yolk
Almond flavoring	

Make a long slit in each date and remove the pits. Mix the almonds and sugar in a bowl. Add several drops of almond flavoring, orange rind, several drops of orange coloring and enough egg yolk to hold ingredients together. Mix well. Turn out onto a board dusted with additional powdered sugar and knead until smooth. Divide into as many even-sized pieces as there are dates and roll each piece into an oblong. Stuff the dates.

Photograph for this recipe on page 145.

GOLDEN ALMONDS

2 c. whole almonds	1 tsp. salt
2 c. sugar	1 tsp. ground nutmeg

Preheat oven to 350 degrees. Spread the almonds in a jelly roll pan. Bake for 10 to 12 minutes. Turn out into another lightly buttered jelly roll pan and keep warm. Place the sugar in a 10-inch heavy skillet and cook over medium heat for about 10 minutes or until sugar changes to a golden liquid, stirring constantly with wooden spoon. Remove from heat and stir in salt and nutmeg quickly, then pour over toasted almonds. Stir to coat each almond. Let stand until cold and turn out on waxed paper. Break into pieces and store between layers of waxed paper in tightly covered container. 1 1/4 pounds.

Evelyn Curtis, Huntsville, Alabama

MOCHA PEANUT CLUSTERS

1/3 c. butter	1 tbsp. instant coffee
1 c. chocolate bits	2 c. chopped salted peanuts
16 marshmallows	

Place butter, chocolate and marshmallows in top of double boiler. Cook over hot water until melted, stirring occasionally. Stir in instant coffee. Remove from heat and stir in the peanuts. Drop by teaspoonfuls onto waxed paper or cookie sheet. Cool. 48 clusters.

Mrs. Sharon Williams, Rome, Georgia

PUDDING PEANUT CLUSTERS

1 pkg. chocolate pudding mix
1 c. sugar
1/2 c. evaporated milk

1 tbsp. butter
1 c. salted peanuts

Combine all ingredients except peanuts in saucepan. Bring to a boil, stirring constantly. Reduce heat and boil gently for 3 minutes, stirring constantly. Remove from heat and add the peanuts, stirring until mixture thickens. Drop from a teaspoon onto cookie sheet. Cool.

Patsy Jordan, Alma, Georgia

FONDANT NUTS

1/3 c. margarine
1/2 c. light corn syrup
1 lb. confectioners' sugar,
    sifted

1 tsp. vanilla
Flavoring
Food coloring
Pecan halves

Mix the margarine, corn syrup and 2 cups sugar in a 3-quart saucepan. Bring to a boil over low heat, stirring constantly. Stir in remaining sugar and vanilla and remove from heat. Stir until mixture holds shape. Pour into a greased baking pan and cool just enough to handle. Knead with lightly greased hands until smooth. Work with a spoon, then knead, if candy hardens too much before kneading. Knead in desired flavoring and coloring. Place small amount of fondant between 2 pecan halves. Centers of pitted prunes, dates or apricots may be filled with fondant or fondant may be shaped as desired.

CREAM PECAN CANDY

4 c. sugar	1 1/2 c. cream or evaporated milk
1 tsp. salt	4 c. pecans, toasted

Combine 2 cups sugar, salt and cream and bring to a boil, stirring until sugar is dissolved. Reduce heat to simmer. Melt remaining sugar in heavy skillet over low heat, stirring constantly. Add to cream mixture and cook to soft-ball stage. Cool to room temperature, then beat until creamy. Add the pecans and drop from teaspoon or pour in buttered dish.

Mrs. Minnie Lee Vaughn, Bay City, Texas

GLAZED PECANS

1/2 lb. pecan halves	
1 c. sugar	3/4 tsp. cinnamon
1/2 c. water	1/4 tsp. nutmeg
1 tsp. salt	1 1/2 tsp. rum flavoring

Place pecans on a baking sheet. Roast in 250-degree oven for 15 minutes. Combine sugar, water, salt and spices in a saucepan and cook to the soft-ball stage. Do not stir. Add flavoring and stir in pecans until creamy and thoroughly coated. Pour onto waxed paper and cool slightly, then separate pecans. Cool thoroughly.

Glenda Barrett, Albany, Georgia

ORANGE-GLAZED PECANS

3/4 c. sugar	1 tsp. grated orange rind
1 tbsp. water	2 1/2 c. pecans
3 tbsp. orange juice	

Combine the sugar, water and orange juice and blend thoroughly. Cook over low heat, stirring occasionally, to 238 degrees on candy thermometer or to soft-ball stage. Remove from heat and add orange rind and pecans. Stir lightly to coat nuts with glaze. Turn out at once onto waxed paper and separate pecans with a fork. Cool completely. Store in covered container in cold place. 2 1/2 cups.

Barbara Calhoun, Macon, Georgia

MEXICAN BROWN SUGAR-PECAN CANDY

4 c. brown sugar	1 c. milk
4 c. pecans	3 tbsp. butter

Combine all ingredients and cook to soft-ball stage. Remove from heat and beat until thick and creamy. Drop by teaspoonfuls onto greased baking sheet. 48 pieces.

Mrs. Richard A. Steele, Lubbock, Texas

PECAN-COCONUT CREAM

1 stick butter, melted
3 c. chopped pecans
1 can sweetened condensed
   milk
2 cans flaked coconut

1 1/2 boxes powdered sugar
1 c. chopped dates
3 6-oz. packages chocolate
   pieces

Combine the butter and pecans and mix well. Add the milk, coconut and powdered sugar and mix thoroughly. Refrigerate for 4 hours. Add the dates to half of the mixture. Roll each mixture into walnut-sized balls. Melt the chocolate pieces in a double boiler and dip the balls in the chocolate. Place on waxed paper until chocolate sets. Store in a cool place.

Mrs. Earl Segrest, Meridian, Mississippi

PRISSY NUTS

2 tsp. instant coffee
1/4 c. sugar
1/4 tsp. cinnamon

2 tbsp. water
Dash of salt
1 1/2 c. pecan halves

Combine all the ingredients in a saucepan and bring to a boil over medium heat. Boil for 3 minutes, stirring constantly. Spread on waxed paper and separate, using 2 forks, then cool.

Mrs. Myrna Parsons, Burleson, Texas

DELICIOUS PRALINES

1 tsp. baking soda
1 c. buttermilk
2 c. sugar
2 tbsp. light corn syrup

1 stick margarine
1 tsp. vanilla
1 1/2 c. pecans

Dissolve the soda in buttermilk, then combine all ingredients except pecans in a deep saucepan. Cook, stirring frequently, to firm-ball stage. Remove from heat and beat until creamy. Add the pecans and drop from a spoon onto waxed paper. 3 dozen.

Mrs. H. R. Selby, Vicksburg, Mississippi

CANDIED HOLIDAY NUTS

2 c. brown sugar
1 c. milk
1 tbsp. margarine

1 tsp. vanilla
Pinch of salt
2 qt. walnuts

Combine the sugar, milk and margarine in a heavy suacepan and cook to soft-ball stage. Add the vanilla and salt. Beat until creamy, then add the walnuts. Stir until walnuts are well coated. Spread on foil and separate. Cool.

Mrs. Jane Proctor, Walnut Ridge, Arkansas

SHERRY PRALINES

2 1/2 c. sugar	2 tbsp. sherry
1/8 tsp. soda	2 c. pecans
1/4 c. light corn syrup	1 tbsp. butter
1/2 c. milk	

Combine the sugar, soda, syrup and milk and cook over medium heat, stirring until sugar is completely dissolved. Cook to 236 degrees on candy thermometer or soft-ball stage. Do not stir. Add sherry, pecans and butter and stir lightly until creamy. Drop by spoonfuls onto waxed paper. 2 dozen.

Mrs. Mabel Lawson, Dothan, Alabama

SUGARED NUTS

2 c. sugar	8 marshmallows
1/2 c. water	1 tsp. vanilla
5 tbsp. light corn syrup	1 qt. nuts

Combine the sugar, water and syrup in a saucepan and cook to 240 degrees on candy thermometer or firm-ball stage. Add the marshmallows and stir until dissolved. Add the vanilla and nuts and stir until sugary. Pour out onto waxed paper and separate with a fork.

Joan Wilf, Walnut Ridge, Arkansas

CANDIED WALNUTS

1 1/2 c. sugar	4 c. walnuts halves
1/4 c. honey	1/2 tsp. vanilla
1/2 c. water	Grated rind of 1 orange

Combine the sugar, honey and water and cook to soft-ball stage. Add the walnuts, vanilla and orange rind and stir carefully until syrup is creamy and thick. Pour onto waxed paper and separate nuts quickly.

Mrs. Ida Hill, Gadsden, Alabama

HOLIDAY RUM BALLS

3 c. crushed vanilla wafers	1 1/2 tbsp. cocoa
1 c. powdered sugar	1 c. chopped walnuts
3 tbsp. corn syrup	6 tbsp. rum

Combine all ingredients and mix together until well blended, adding drops of hot water if needed to hold together. Pinch off small pieces of the mixture and roll into small balls. Roll in additional powdered sugar and store in covered container for 1 or 2 days to ripen.

Mrs. Sylvia Washburn, Johnson City, Tennessee

SOUR CREAM NUTS

1 c. sugar
1/3 c. sour cream
1 tsp. light corn syrup

2 tbsp. butter
1 tsp. vanilla
2 c. nuts

Combine the sugar, sour cream and syrup in a saucepan and cover. Bring to a boil and cook over low heat to soft-ball stage. Add the butter and vanilla and cool to lukewarm. Beat until mixture loses gloss. Add nuts quickly and stir until coated. Spread on foil. Break apart when cool. Store in a container with a tight-fitting lid.

Mrs. Jerome Smith, Paducah, Kentucky

GLACE NUTS

1 1/2 c. sugar
1/2 c. light or dark corn
   syrup
1/2 c. water

1/2 tsp. salt
3 c. nuts
2 tbsp. margarine
1 tsp. vanilla

Combine the sugar, corn syrup, water and salt in a heavy saucepan and cook over low heat, stirring constantly, until sugar is dissolved. Cook over medium heat, without stirring, until mixture reaches 300 degrees on a candy thermometer or until a small amount of mixture dropped into cold water separates into threads which are hard and brittle. Spread the nuts in a shallow pan. Bake in 350-degree oven for 10 minutes. Reduce heat under syrup mixture to very low, then add nuts, margarine and vanilla. Stir just until nuts are coated and margarine is melted. Remove from heat and turn out into a large, coarse sieve placed over greased pan. Let excess syrup drain off for about 1 minute. Spread nuts out in a greased large, shallow pan or baking sheet, using forks to separate. Cool excess syrup mixture, break into pieces and serve as hard candy. Saucepan may be placed over boiling water and nuts removed with forks, if preferred. Spread out on large greased pan. Spiced glace nuts may be prepared by omitting vanilla and combining 1 teaspoon cinnamon, 1/4 teaspoon cloves, 1/8 teaspoon nutmeg and 1/8 teaspoon ginger with sugar mixture before cooking.

poured & hard candies

Poured and hard candies are so crunchy or chewy, they're alternately referred to as "jaw breakers" or "all day candies." Children love them for their long-lasting qualities, and homemakers have found that they're easy to store.

Women from America's Southland who cook to please their families have developed many flavorful candy recipes. Some are traditional favorites, like the one you'll find for Golden Peanut Brittle. Others are imports from outside the South which have become favorites over the years — like Atlantic City Taffy. But all have that taste and texture which make them such delights.

Just imagine how entranced your tiny guest will be when you serve Never-fail Caramels at the next children's party you give. And Five-Pound Fudge may be just the recipe you've needed for the next food sale at your church or school. If holiday time is approaching, feature Christmas Walnut Toffee — it's Old English in its origins, but good candy recipes are timeless!

Be an innovative candy maker . . . explore the pages of this marvelous section. You'll soon be planning your next adventure into the wonderful world of poured and hard candies — an adventure that's certain to pay dividends of good flavor for you and your family!

157

CARAMEL POPCORN

1/4 c. corn oil	1 c. dark corn syrup
1/2 c. popcorn	1 c. sugar
1 c. salted peanuts or cashew	1/4 c. water
nuts	1/4 c. margarine

Heat the oil in a 4-quart kettle over medium heat for 3 minutes. Add the popcorn and cover, leaving small air space at edge of cover. Shake frequently over medium heat until popping stops. Place the popcorn in a large, greased heat-resistant bowl and add peanuts. Bake in 300-degree oven until syrup is prepared. Combine the corn syrup, sugar, water and margarine in a heavy 2-quart saucepan and bring to a boil over medium heat, stirring constantly. Cook, stirring occasionally, to 280 degrees on a candy thermometer or until small amount of syrup dropped into cold water separates into threads which are hard but not brittle. Remove popcorn mixture from oven and pour syrup over mixture gradually, stirring quickly until kernels are evenly coated. Spread on 2 greased baking sheets and spread out into thin layer with greased hands. Cool, then separate into clusters. Store in tightly covered container. About 1 1/2 pounds.

Photograph for this recipe on page 156.

NEVER-FAIL CARAMELS

2 c. sugar	1 tsp. vanilla
1 2/3 c. white corn syrup	1 c. chopped nuts (opt.)
1 c. butter or margarine	2 c. evaporated milk

Combine all the ingredients except 1 cup milk and bring to a boil. Add the remaining milk, 1 tablespoon at a time and keep boiling, stirring constantly, until mixture forms a soft ball when a small amount is dropped in cold water. Pour into a greased pan and cool. Cut into squares and wrap each piece in waxed paper. 2 pounds.

Mrs. George Champion, Harrodsburg, Kentucky

CARAMELS

1 1/4 c. (packed) brown sugar	1 c. evaporated milk
1/2 c. sugar	1/2 tsp. vanilla
1 1/3 c. dark corn syrup	1/8 tsp. salt
6 tbsp. butter	2 c. chopped nuts

Combine the sugars and syrup in a heavy saucepan. Cook over medium heat, stirring constantly, to 245 degrees on candy thermometer or to the firm-ball stage. Stir in the butter, then add the milk slowly. Cook again to 245 degrees. Remove from heat and add vanilla and salt. Pour into a greased 13 x 9 x 2-inch pan and cool until firm. Spread nuts on buttered waxed paper and turn the candy out on top of the nuts. Roll as for jelly roll, pressing the nuts into caramel, then wrap in plastic wrap. Slice to serve. 3 dozen pieces.

Mrs. Hamilton Grundy, Chattanooga, Tennessee

CHOCOLATE MINT DROPS

1 1/3 c. sugar
1/2 c. water
1 tsp. glycerin

2 drops of oil of peppermint
2 sq. semisweet chocolate

Combine the sugar and water in 2-quart heavy saucepan and cook slowly, stirring constantly, until sugar is dissolved. Bring to a boil without stirring, then blend in glycerin until just mixed. Cover the saucepan and cook for 3 minutes. Uncover and cook over low heat to 240 degrees on candy thermometer or to the soft-ball stage. Remove from heat and add the oil of peppermint, stirring to just mix. Pour onto oiled baking sheet. Work with oiled knife or spatula until candy is smooth and creamy. Roll quickly into 3/4-inch balls, then flatten with knife. Place on oiled baking sheet. Melt the chocolate and drop on top of each peppermint candy.

Mrs. Erika Benton, Fort Smith, Arkansas

MUNCHING BRITTLE

1/2 lb. shelled peanuts
2 c. sugar

1/4 tsp. cream of tartar

Place the peanuts in a baking pan. Bake at 350 degrees for 10 minutes. Remove from oven and rub off all the skins. Keep the peanuts hot. Place the sugar in a heavy saucepan over a low heat and stir until melted. Dissolve the cream of tartar in small amount of warm water and stir into melted sugar slowly. Cook, without stirring, until the syrup is golden brown. Add the hot nuts. Do not stir or mixture will grain. Pour immediately onto a sheet of greased foil and distribute the peanuts gently and evenly with a greased fork. Cool thoroughly and break into pieces. Store in an airtight container.

QUICK CHOCOLATE FUDGE

1/4 c. margarine	1/2 c. light or dark corn syrup
3 oz. unsweetened chocolate	1 tbsp. water
1 lb. confectioners' sugar	1 tsp. vanilla
1/3 c. instant nonfat dry milk	1/2 c. chopped nuts (opt.)

Melt the margarine and chocolate in a saucepan over low heat or in top of a 2-quart double boiler over boiling water. Sift confectioners' sugar and nonfat dry milk together and set aside. Stir corn syrup, water and vanilla into chocolate mixture. Blend in sifted ingredients in 2 additions, stirring until well blended and smooth. Remove from boiling water and mix in nuts. Turn into a greased 8-inch square pan. Cool and cut into squares. Blonde fudge may be made by omitting chocolate and water, using light corn syrup and increasing vanilla to 2 teaspoons. One cup miniature marshmallows may be substituted for nuts.

BROWN SUGAR FUDGE

1 c. (packed) light brown sugar	1 tbsp. butter
1 c. sugar	1 tsp. vanilla
3/4 c. milk	1/2 c. chopped walnuts

Combine the sugars and milk in a heavy saucepan and cook over medium heat to soft-ball stage, stirring occasionally. Remove from heat, then add the butter and vanilla. Place saucepan in cold water and beat until very thick. Add the walnuts and pour into a greased 9-inch square pan. Refrigerate until set, then cut into squares.

Mrs. Neale O. Westfall, Portsmouth, Virginia

CHOCOLATE FUDGE WITH CHERRIES

4 c. sugar	1 pt. marshmallow creme
1/4 c. butter or margarine	1/2 c. chopped nuts
1 can evaporated milk	1/2 c. chopped candied
3 6-oz. packages chocolate	cherries
pieces	

Combine the sugar, butter and milk in a heavy saucepan and bring to a boil over medium heat, stirring gently. Boil for 5 minutes, then add the remaining ingredients and stir until thoroughly blended. Pour into 2 large pans and refrigerate overnight. Cut into squares.

Mrs. Blanche Jeffers, Bridgeport, West Virginia

PEANUT SCOTCH FUDGE

2 6-oz. packages butterscotch	1/2 c. peanut butter
morsels	1 tsp. vanilla
1 14-oz. can sweetened	1/8 tsp. salt
condensed milk	Candied cherries, cut in
16 marshmallows	quarters

Combine the butterscotch morsels, milk and marshmallows in top of a double boiler. Place over boiling water and stir occasionally until melted and smooth. Remove from heat. Stir in the peanut butter, vanilla and salt and pour into a buttered 8-inch square pan. Chill until almost firm. Mark into squares and press cherry quarter on each square. About 2 1/4 pounds.

Photograph for this recipe on page 1.

DOUBLE FLAVOR FUDGE

2 c. evaporated milk	1 6-oz. package semisweet
4 1/2 c. sugar	chocolate morsels
1/2 tsp. salt	2 c. chopped California
1/2 c. butter or margarine	walnuts
32 marshmallows	1 6-oz. package butterscotch
2 tsp. vanilla	morsels

Combine 1 cup milk, 2 1/4 cups sugar, 1/4 teaspoon salt, 1/4 cup butter and 16 marshmallows in a 2-quart saucepan and bring to a boil, stirring constantly. Continue to boil, stirring constantly, for 5 minutes and remove from heat. Stir in 1 teaspoon vanilla and the chocolate morsels until smooth. Add 1 cup walnuts and mix. Pour into 2 waxed paper or foil-lined 8-inch square pans. Combine remaining milk, sugar, salt, butter and marshmallows in a 2-quart saucepan and bring to a boil, stirring constantly. Continue to boil, stirring constantly, for 5 minutes and remove from heat. Stir in the butterscotch morsels and remaining vanilla until smooth. Add remaining walnuts and mix. Spread over chocolate layers and chill until firm. Cut into 1 1/4-inch pieces. Top with walnut halves, if desired. Two cups marshmallow creme may be substituted for marshmallows.

Photograph for this recipe on page 5.

MEXICAN SKILLET FUDGE

2 c. sugar	1/2 c. miniature marshmallows
3 tbsp. butter	1 1/2 c. semisweet chocolate
1 tsp. cinnamon	pieces
1/2 tsp. salt	2/3 c. chopped pecans
1 c. evaporated milk	1 tsp. vanilla

Combine the sugar, butter, cinnamon, salt and evaporated milk in an electric skillet and set the thermostat at 280 degrees. Bring mixture to a boil and boil for 5 minutes, stirring constantly. Turn off skillet. Add the marshmallows, chocolate pieces, pecans and vanilla. Stir until marshmallows and chocolate are melted and smoothly blended. Pour into a buttered 8-inch square pan. Cool, then cut into squares. 2 pounds.

Mrs. Ray McLean, Alexandria, Virginia

OATMEAL FUDGE

5 tbsp. cocoa	1/2 c. peanut butter
2 3/4 c. sugar	3 c. rolled oats
1/2 c. margarine	1 tsp. vanilla
1/2 c. milk	

Combine the cocoa, sugar, margarine and milk in a saucepan and boil for 2 minutes. Remove from heat and add the peanut butter, oats and vanilla. Mix well and pour into a waxed paper-lined pan. Cool and cut into squares.

Mrs. Frances Stone, Huntington, West Virginia

FIVE-POUND FUDGE

1 can evaporated milk	2 pkg. chocolate pieces
4 c. sugar	1 c. chopped nuts
1 lb. sweet chocolate, cut up	1 pt. marshmallow creme

Combine the milk and sugar in a heavy saucepan and boil for 4 minutes. Add the remaining ingredients and stir until well blended. Pour into pan and chill, then cut into squares.

Mrs. Marian Davis, Norfolk, Virginia

TRIPLE-DECKER FUDGE

2 6-oz. packages butterscotch	2 c. miniature marshmallows
pieces	2 6-oz. packages chocolate
2 tbsp. butter	pieces
1 c. chopped walnuts	

Melt the butterscotch pieces and 1 tablespoon butter over hot water. Spread in a buttered 9-inch square pan. Press the walnuts on top. Cover with an even layer of marshmallows, pressing gently into surface. Melt the chocolate and remaining butter over hot water, then spread evenly over marshmallow layer. Cool. Cut into squares before candy is completely firm.

Mrs. Bob Rogers, Lexington, Kentucky

JELLIED MARSHMALLOW SQUARES

1 pkg. cherry gelatin	1/4 c. light corn syrup
2/3 c. hot water	Powdered sugar
1 c. sugar	

Dissolve the gelatin in hot water over low heat, then add the sugar and stir until dissolved. Mix in the syrup and chill until slightly thickened. Beat for about 5 minutes or until stiff. Pour into an 8 x 8 x 2-inch waxed paper-lined pan and chill overnight. Turn mixture with waxed paper onto board heavily dusted with powdered sugar, then moisten paper with damp sponge and let stand for several minutes. Peel off paper and dust top with powdered sugar. Cut into squares and then roll edges in sugar.

Mrs. William C. Boyd, Atlanta, Georgia

NUT GOODIE CANDY BARS

1 12-oz. package chocolate pieces	1 c. peanut butter
2 6-oz. packages butterscotch pieces	1 lb. miniature marshmallows
	1 1/2 c. Spanish peanuts

Combine the chocolate and butterscotch and melt over low heat. Add the peanut butter and stir until well blended. Stir in the marshmallows and peanuts, then pour into a buttered 12 x 15-inch pan. Cut into bars; store in refrigerator.

Mrs. Deborah King, Dothan, Alabama

POURED FONDANT

2 c. sugar	1/2 c. water
1/3 c. light corn syrup	1/8 tsp. cream of tartar

Combine all the ingredients in a 2-quart heavy saucepan. Cook over medium heat, stirring constantly until sugar dissolves and mixture comes to a boil. Cover the saucepan and cook for 3 minutes, then remove the cover and cook without stirring to 340 degrees on candy thermometer or to the soft-ball stage. Wipe sugar crystals from side of pan. Remove from heat and pour at once onto a cold, slightly wet platter or baking sheet. Cool until center of candy feels lukewarm. Beat with a spatula until white and creamy, then knead with hands until smooth. Shape into a ball. Store in a covered dish in refrigerator for at least 2 or 3 days before using. Shape into desired shapes.

Mrs. Joann Cummings, Norfolk, Virginia

ATLANTIC CITY TAFFY

2 c. sugar	2 tsp. glycerin
1 c. light corn syrup	2 tbsp. butter
1 1/2 c. water	2 tsp. vanilla
1 1/2 tsp. salt	

Combine the sugar, syrup, water, salt and glycerin in a 3-quart heavy saucepan. Place over low heat and stir until sugar dissolves, then cook without stirring to 260 degrees on candy thermometer or to the hard-ball stage. Remove from the heat and add the butter, stirring until butter is melted. Pour into a buttered 13 x 9-inch shallow pan. Cool until easily handled, then gather into a ball and pull until rather firm. Add the vanilla while pulling, then stretch out into a long rope and cut in 1 or 2-inch pieces. Wrap each piece in waxed paper when hard and twist paper at both ends. 1 1/4 pounds.

Mrs. Edith Edmonson, Winter Haven, Florida

PEANUT BUTTER TAFFY

3/4 c. sugar	1/3 c. water
1 c. maple syrup	2 oz. chocolate, melted
1/2 c. corn syrup	1/4 c. peanut butter
1/4 tsp. salt	

Combine the sugar, syrups, salt and water and cook over low heat, stirring constantly, until sugar is dissolved. Cook to 238 degrees on candy thermometer or soft-crack stage, then add the chocolate. Pour into a greased pan and cool until easily handled. Pull until almost firm, then spread with the peanut butter. Fold over and pull enough to mix peanut butter thoroughly with candy. Cut into parts and wrap each piece in waxed paper.

Ida McFarlane, Bridgeport, Alabama

PEANUT BRITTLE

1 c. light or dark corn syrup	2 tbsp. margarine
1 c. sugar	1 1/2 c. salted peanuts
1/4 c. water	1 tsp. soda

Combine the corn syrup, sugar, water and margarine in a heavy 2-quart saucepan. Bring to a boil over medium heat, stirring constantly until sugar is dissolved. Cook, without stirring, to 280 degrees on a candy thermometer or until a small amount of mixture dropped into cold water separates into threads which are hard but not brittle. Stir in peanuts gradually so mixture continues to boil. Cook, stirring frequently, to 300 degrees or until small amount of mixture dropped into cold water separates into threads which are hard and brittle. Remove from heat. Add the soda and blend quickly, but thoroughly. Turn onto heavily greased baking sheet immediately and spread evenly to edges of baking sheet with a greased metal spatula. Cool, then break into pieces. 1 1/2 pounds.

Photograph for this recipe on page 156.

ALMOND BUTTER CRUNCH

1 1/2 c. blanched almonds	1 1/2 c. sugar
Butter	1 tbsp. light corn syrup
1/2 tsp. salt	

Preheat oven to 450 degrees. Place the almonds in a saucepan and add enough water to cover. Bring to a boil and reduce heat. Simmer for 2 minutes, then drain. Split almonds with a paring knife. Melt 2 tablespoons butter in a 15 1/2 x 10 1/2 x 1-inch jelly roll pan and add the almonds and salt. Bake for 8 to 10 minutes, stirring occasionally. Remove from oven and spread almonds evenly in pan. Melt 3/4 cup butter in a 2-quart saucepan and stir in the sugar, corn syrup and 3 tablespoons water. Cook, without stirring, to hard-crack stage or 240 degrees on candy thermometer. Remove from heat and pour in thin stream over almonds. Cool and break into pieces.

MOLASSES-PEANUT BRITTLE

2 c. sugar	2 tbsp. butter
1 c. light corn syrup	2 c. salted peanuts
1/2 c. water	1 tbsp. soda
1/4 c. dark molasses	

Combine the sugar, syrup and water in a 3-quart saucepan and bring to a boil, stirring until sugar is dissolved. Cook to hard-crack stage or to 290 degrees on a candy thermometer. Stir in molasses and butter and cook for 30 seconds longer. Remove from heat and stir in peanuts and soda quickly. Mix thoroughly and pour immediately into large, buttered cookie pan. Cool, then break into pieces. Yield: 2 pounds.

Mrs. Glenn Harris, Jennings, Louisiana

ALMOND BRITTLE

1 c. blanched almonds	2 tbsp. butter
1/2 c. sugar	Salt

Combine the almonds, sugar and butter and cook over medium heat for 10 to 12 minutes or until color changes, stirring constantly. Pour onto buttered foil and sprinkle lightly with salt. Cool, then break into pieces.

Mrs. Franklin Knox, New Orleans, Louisiana

TEMPTING PEANUT BRITTLE

2 c. sugar	3 tbsp. butter or margarine
1 c. light corn syrup	1 tsp. vanilla
1/4 c. water	2 tsp. soda
1 1/2 c. salted peanuts	

Combine the sugar, corn syrup and water in a 3-quart heavy saucepan and mix well. Cook over medium heat, stirring constantly, until sugar dissolves. Cook, stirring frequently, to 285 degrees on a candy thermometer. Remove from heat and stir in the peanuts and butter. Cook, stirring constantly, to 295 degrees. Remove from heat. Add the vanilla and soda and stir quickly to blend. Mixture will foam. Pour onto a well-buttered marble slab or 2 large buttered baking sheets and spread out thin. Cool for 5 minutes or just long enough to handle. Turn candy over and pull to stretch as thin as possible. Cool thoroughly and break in pieces. About 2 pounds.

Photograph for this recipe on page 2.

FILBERT BRITTLE

2 c. sugar	1 c. coarsely chopped filberts
1/2 lb. butter	

Combine the sugar and butter in a skillet and cook slowly, stirring constantly with a fork until golden brown. Add the filberts and bring to a boil. Remove from heat and pour onto a buttered baking sheet, spreading with a fork. Cool, then break into pieces.

Mrs. Inez Patter, Albany, Georgia

GOLDEN PEANUT BRITTLE

1 1/2 c. sugar	2 c. peanuts
1/2 c. hot water	1/4 c. butter
1/2 c. light corn syrup	3 tsp. soda

Mix the sugar, water and corn syrup in a saucepan and cook over medium heat until mixture spins a thread. Add the peanuts and reduce heat. Cook until golden brown. Remove from heat. Add butter and soda and mix well. Pour into greased jelly roll pan and cool. Break into pieces.

Mrs. Maebelle Deal, Headland, Alabama

PECAN BRITTLE

2 c. chopped pecans	**1/4 tsp. soda**
2 c. sugar	**1 tsp. vanilla**
1/4 tsp. salt	

Spread the pecans on a buttered cookie sheet. Cook the sugar in iron skillet until golden brown, stirring constantly. Remove from heat. Mix the salt, soda and vanilla and stir into melted sugar. Pour over pecans immediately and cool. Break into pieces.

Juanita Fuller, Jonesboro, Arkansas

TWO-TONE TRUFFLES

1 1/2 c. chopped nuts	**1 1/2 c. chocolate pieces**
1 1/2 c. powdered sugar	**3/4 c. sweetened condensed**
1 egg white	**milk**
1 tbsp. rum extract	**1 tbsp. butter**

Combine the nuts, sugar, egg white and rum and mix well. Spread in a buttered, waxed paper-lined pan. Melt the chocolate and stir in the milk and butter. Cook for about 5 minutes or until thick, then pour over the nut mixture. Cool until firm, then cut into squares. Wrap each piece in plastic wrap.

Dana Ray Owens, Eldorado, Texas

ANISE CANDY

2 c. sugar	**1/2 tsp. food coloring**
1 c. corn syrup	**1 1/2 tsp. anise flavoring**
1/2 c. water	

Combine the sugar, syrup and water and cook to the hard-crack stage. Add the food coloring and flavoring. Pour into a buttered 8-inch square pan. Cool, then break into pieces.

Mrs. Helen Marshall, El Paso, Texas

HARD PEANUT BRITTLE

2 c. sugar	**1 c. coarsely chopped peanuts**
2 tsp. butter	

Melt the sugar in a heavy frying pan over moderate heat, stirring constantly, until golden brown. Remove from heat and stir in the butter. Spread the peanuts in a shallow, well-buttered pan and pour sugar mixture over peanuts. Cool until hardened and break into pieces.

Mrs. J. B. Seigler, Seabrook, South Carolina

SUPREME PEANUT BRITTLE

3 c. sugar	2 tbsp. butter
1/2 c. water	2 tsp. soda
1 c. white corn syrup	1 tsp. salt
3 c. peanuts	1 3 1/2-oz. can flaked coconut

Mix the sugar, water and corn syrup in a saucepan and cook until mixture spins a thread. Add peanuts and cook, stirring constantly, until golden brown. Remove from heat. Add the butter, soda, salt, and coconut and mix thoroughly. Pour out on a large sheet of buttered foil. Cool until hardened and break into pieces.

Mrs. R. L. Quigley, Bridge City, Texas

TWO POUNDS OF PEANUT BRITTLE

2 c. sugar	1 tsp. soda
1 c. light corn syrup	1 tsp. salt
1/4 c. water	1 tsp. vinegar
2 c. peanuts	

Combine the sugar, corn syrup and water in a saucepan and cook to soft-ball stage. Add peanuts and cook to hard-crack stage. Remove from heat and add soda, salt and vinegar. Stir well and pour into a buttered cookie pan. Cool and break into pieces.

Mrs. Kenneth Speer, Jal, New Mexico

BUTTER BRICKLE CANDY

1 c. butter	1 c. sugar
2 tbsp. water	6 chocolate bars, crushed

Combine the butter, water and sugar in a skillet and cook over medium heat, stirring constantly, until golden brown. Pour into buttered 9-inch pan. Cover with chocolate candy. Cool until hardened, then break into pieces.

Mrs. Grover Parham, Orlando, Florida

HARD ALMOND CANDY

1 c. sugar	1 c. half and half
1 c. dark corn syrup	1 c. chopped blanched almonds
1/3 c. butter	

Combine the sugar, corn syrup, butter and half and half in a 2-quart heavy saucepan and place over low heat, stirring until sugar dissolves. Cook, stirring occasionally, to hard-ball stage or 250 degrees on candy thermometer. Remove from heat and add almonds. Pour into 1 1/2-inch fluted paper dessert cups or drop from teaspoon onto waxed paper. Cool.

Mrs. Bart Warren, Charlotte, North Carolina

BUTTER CRUNCH

1 c. margarine	1 tbsp. light corn syrup
1 c. sugar	3/4 c. finely chopped nuts
2 tbsp. water	4 oz. semisweet chocolate

Melt the margarine in a 2-quart saucepan over low heat. Remove from heat. Add the sugar and stir until well blended. Add water and corn syrup and mix well. Cook over low heat, stirring frequently, to hard-crack stage or 290 degrees on candy thermometer. Remove from heat. Stir in the nuts and pour into lightly greased cookie pan. Cool until hardened. Melt the chocolate over boiling water. Spread half the chocolate over candy and cool until firm. Spread remaining chocolate over other side and cool. Break in pieces. Store in tightly covered container.

Mrs. Wanda Brian, Weatherford, Texas

BUTTER-ALMOND TOFFEE

1 c. chopped roasted unblanched almonds	1/3 c. (packed) brown sugar
1 c. butter	2 tbsp. water
1 c. sugar	1/2 tsp. soda
	3 oz. semisweet chocolate bits

Sprinkle half the almonds on a greased 9 x 13-inch pan. Melt the butter in a heavy saucepan. Add the sugars and water and mix well. Bring to a boil, stirring constantly. Cook to 300 degrees on candy thermometer or hard-crack stage. Remove from heat and stir in soda quickly. Pour carefully over almonds in pan and let cool for about 5 minutes. Sprinkle chocolate bits over toffee and spread out evenly. Heat of candy will melt chocolate. Sprinkle remaining almonds over chocolate and press in lightly. Cool, then break into pieces. About 1 1/2 pounds.

CANDY HEARTS

1 c. sugar	3/4 tsp. peppermint extract
1/2 c. light corn syrup	Red food coloring
1/4 c. water	Confectioners' sugar frosting
Corn oil	

Mix the sugar, corn syrup and water in a saucepan. Cook over medium heat, stirring constantly, until mixture boils and sugar is dissolved. Boil, without stirring, to 295 degrees on a candy thermometer or until small amount of mixture dropped into very cold water separates into hard threads. Arrange greased heart-shaped molds or other molds of various sizes on greased baking sheets. Remove syrup from heat and stir in the peppermint extract and desired amount of red food coloring. Pour into molds immediately to depth of 1/8 inch and cool until candy is hard. Remove from molds and decorate with confectioners' sugar frosting. Lemon extract and yellow food coloring or spearmint extract and green food coloring may be substituted for peppermint extract and red food coloring. About 12 candy shapes.

ENGLISH TOFFEE

1 c. sugar	1 tsp. vanilla
1 c. butter	1 8-oz. chocolate bar
3 tbsp. water	3/4 c. finely chopped pecans

Combine the sugar, butter and water in a saucepan and cook to hard-crack stage or 300 degrees on candy thermometer, stirring constantly. Add vanilla and pour into a buttered 9 x 9-inch pan. Place chocolate bar on top and spread evenly when melted. Sprinkle pecans over top. Cool thoroughly and break into pieces.

Mary E. West, Greensboro, North Carolina

ALMOND TOFFEE

1 lb. butter or margarine	1 12-oz. package chocolate
2 c. sugar	pieces
1 c. unblanched almonds	Chopped pecans

Mix the butter, sugar and almonds in a saucepan and cook to hard-crack stage or 290 degrees on a candy thermometer, stirring constantly. Pour into a jelly roll pan. Melt the chocolate and spread half the chocolate over candy. Sprinkle with pecans. Cool until hardened. Turn over and spread with remaining chocolate. Sprinkle with pecans. Break into pieces. Cashew nuts may be substituted for almonds.

Mrs. Sidney A. Stephens, Fort Worth, Texas

CHRISTMAS WALNUT TOFFEE

1 c. butter	1 1/2 c. chopped walnuts
1 c. sugar	1 6-oz. package chocolate
1 tbsp. light corn syrup	pieces
3 tbsp. water	

Melt the butter in a 2-quart saucepan and stir in sugar gradually. Add the corn syrup and water and cook over moderate heat, stirring occasionally, to hard-crack stage. Add 1 cup walnuts and cook for 3 minutes longer, stirring constantly. Pour into buttered 9-inch square pan and cool until hardened. Remove from pan and place on waxed paper. Melt chocolate pieces. Coat one side of toffee with half the chocolate and sprinkle with half the remaining walnuts. Cool. Turn toffee and spread with remaining chocolate. Sprinkle with remaining walnuts. Break into pieces.

Mrs. Catherine May, Charleston, West Virginia

ENGLISH ALMOND TOFFEE

1 c. chopped almonds	1 c. (packed) brown sugar
1 c. butter	1 8-oz. chocolate bar

Sprinkle 1/2 cup almonds in greased 9 x 12-inch pan. Melt the butter in saucepan. Add the sugar and mix well. Boil for 12 minutes, stirring constantly. Add remaining almonds and pour over almonds in pan. Place chocolate on top and spread to cover when melted.

Mrs. Earl Durham, Cape Charles, Virginia

RED CINNAMON CANDY

2 3/4 c. sugar	1 tsp. (scant) oil of
3/4 c. light corn syrup	cinnamon
3/4 c. water	1 tsp. red food coloring

Combine the sugar, corn syrup and water in a saucepan and cook to hard-crack stage. Remove from heat and stir in oil of cinnamon and food coloring. Pour into a greased 9 x 13-inch pan. Cool until hardened and break into pieces.

Mrs. Sarah Wooten, Baltimore, Maryland

candies for small cooks

Can you still remember the first time you prepared a batch of fudge? The careful way you followed directions ... the excited watching while the fudge cooled in the cooking pan ... the constant stirring until it lost its gloss ... then the waiting while it hardened in the dish. All that energy was well spent when you tasted the first bite of fudge you had made yourself!

Let this wonderful experience be part of your children's memories — with the help of the recipes you'll find in the following section. These are recipes especially chosen because they are appropriate for small cooks. All the chance has been cooked out long ago, leaving only home-tested favorites proven successful in homes throughout the South. The ingredients are simple and few; the directions are easy-to-follow.

Imagine how excited your children will be when they prepare candies for Halloween — Caramel Apples, Popcorn Balls, and many more. There are even recipes for old-fashioned Pull Taffy — that delight of children a hundred years ago.

On the next rainy day when your children are asking for something to do, why not turn to these pages. You'll find yourself sharing an unforgettable experience with them as they suddenly become small cooks with the large responsibility of preparing their very own batch of candy!

CANDY APPLES

8 med. red apples	1 1 3/4-oz. bottle red
2 c. sugar	cinnamon candies
1 c. light corn syrup	10 drops of red food coloring (opt.)
1/2 c. water	

Wash and dry the apples. Remove stems and insert wooden skewers or spoons into stem ends. Combine the sugar, corn syrup and water in a heavy 2-quart saucepan. Cook over medium heat, stirring constantly, until mixture boils and sugar is dissolved. Cook, without stirring, to 250 degrees on candy thermometer or until small amount dropped into very cold water forms hard ball. Add the cinnamon candies and cook to 285 degrees or until small amount dropped into very cold water separates into hard threads. Remove from heat and stir in food coloring. Hold each apple by skewer and twirl in syrup quickly, tilting pan to cover apple with syrup. Remove apple from syrup and allow excess to drip off. Twirl to spread syrup smoothly over apple and place on lightly greased baking sheet to cool. Store in cool place. Syrup may be reheated over low heat if mixture cools too quickly.

APPLE JEWELS

12 env. unflavored gelatin	1/2 c. orange juice
2 c. apple juice	2 tbsp. grated orange rind
4 c. canned applesauce	1 tsp. ginger
1 tsp. salt	Yellow food coloring
6 c. sugar	4 tsp. lime juice
1/4 c. lemon juice	Green food coloring
4 tsp. grated lemon rind	2 tbsp. cinnamon candies

174

Soften the gelatin in apple juice in a bowl. Combine the applesauce, salt, sugar, lemon juice and rind and orange juice and rind in a saucepan and bring to a boil. Add the gelatin and stir until dissolved. Simmer for 20 minutes. Divide into 3 parts. Add the ginger and several drops of yellow food coloring to 1 part. Add the lime juice and several drops of green food coloring to second part. Add the cinnamon candies to remaining part and stir until dissolved. Pour each mixture into an 8 x 8 x 2-inch pan and chill for at least 4 hours or until set. Cut into decorative shapes with canape cutters or the inside of a doughnut cutter and roll in additional sugar. Candies will keep for several weeks in a covered container in the refrigerator. 6 dozen candies.

Photograph for this recipe on page 172.

CARAMEL APPLES

6 med, apples	1 can sweetened condensed milk
1 c. sugar	1/4 tsp. salt
1/2 c. light corn syrup	1/2 tsp. maple flavoring

Wash and dry the apples and insert a wooden skewer in stem end of each apple. Combine remaining ingredients in a saucepan and place over low heat. Cook, stirring constantly, to soft-ball stage or to 230 degrees on candy thermometer. Remove from heat and let stand until mixture stops bubbling. Dip each apple into milk mixture and swirl until well coated. Place apples, skewer side up, on a buttered dish or waxed paper and cool.

Mrs. Fletcher Jernigan, Raleigh, North Carolina

RED CANDY APPLES

8 med. apples	1/2 c. water
1 c. sugar	1/2 c. red cinnamon candies
1 c. light corn syrup	

Wash and dry the apples and insert a wooden stick into stem end of each apple. Mix remaining ingredients in a saucepan and cook to hard-crack stage. Dip apples into syrup quickly and place on greased waxed paper. Cool.

Delores Kennedy, Columbia, South Carolina

EASY CHOCOLATE-DIPPED FONDANT

2 1-lb. boxes powdered sugar	1 can flaked coconut
2 sticks butter, melted	1 12-oz. package semisweet
1 can sweetened condensed milk	chocolate pieces
1 lb. chopped pecans	1 cake paraffin

Combine the sugar, butter, milk, pecans and coconut in a bowl and shape into small balls. Chill. Melt the chocolate and paraffin in a double boiler. Dip the balls into chocolate mixture and place on waxed paper to cool.

Martha McCurry, Lipan, Texas

CHOCOLATE-COVERED CANDY

1/2 c. butter or margarine	2 6-oz. packages chocolate
2 lb. powdered sugar	pieces
2 c. shredded coconut	2 6-oz. packages German's
4 c. chopped pecans	sweet chocolate
1 tsp. vanilla	1 stick paraffin
1 can sweetened condensed milk	

Melt the butter and pour into a large bowl. Add the sugar, coconut, pecans, vanilla and milk and mix well. Chill for 15 minutes. Shape into small balls and chill. Place remaining ingredients in a double boiler and heat until melted. Dip balls in chocolate mixture with a fork and place on waxed paper until chocolate hardens.

Mrs. James Aikens, Fort Knox, Kentucky

NUT FUDGE

1 can sweetened condensed milk	1 tsp. vanilla
1 c. sugar	1 c. chopped nuts
1/4 c. milk	

Combine first 3 ingredients in a saucepan. Cook over medium heat, stirring constantly with a wooden spoon, until mixture leaves side of the saucepan and forms a ball. Remove from heat. Add vanilla and nuts and beat until thick. Spread in a buttered dish and cool. Cut in squares.

Mrs. Cherrie Y. Manuel, Mamou, Louisiana

CREAMY ROLLED FUDGE

2 tbsp. butter	1/2 tsp. vanilla
1 1/2 sq. chocolate	Pinch of salt
2 c. sugar	Chopped nuts to taste (opt.)
1 c. milk	

Melt the butter and chocolate in a saucepan over low heat. Add the sugar and mix thoroughly. Add milk and bring to a boil, stirring constantly. Cook to soft-ball stage and remove from heat. Cool until bottom of saucepan is just warm. Add vanilla, salt and nuts and beat until mixture loses gloss. Shape into rolls and place on waxed paper.

Mrs. O. Bruce, Columbus, Mississippi

PEANUT BUTTER-CHOCOLATE FUDGE

2 c. sugar	1 tsp. vanilla
3 tbsp. cocoa	1 c. peanut butter
1/2 c. cream	

Combine the sugar and cocoa in a saucepan and stir in the cream. Bring to a boil and cook for 3 minutes. Remove from heat. Add the vanilla and peanut butter and beat until smooth. Drop by teaspoonfuls on waxed paper and cool.

Mrs. J. Millard Tawes, Annapolis, Maryland

PEANUT BUTTER FUDGE SUPREME

2 c. sugar	1 c. peanut butter
2/3 c. milk	1 tsp. vanilla
1 pt. marshmallow creme	

Mix the sugar and milk in a saucepan and cook to soft-ball stage. Remove from heat. Add the marshmallow creme, peanut butter and vanilla and mix well. Pour into buttered 6 x 10-inch pan and cut into 2-inch squares. 2 pounds.

Lois Plott, San Angelo, Texas

PULLED MINT CANDY

2 c. sugar	Oil of peppermint or
1 stick butter or margarine	wintergreen to taste
1/2 c. water	4 drops of food coloring

Combine sugar, butter and water in a heavy saucepan. Cook over low heat, stirring with a wooden spoon, until sugar is dissolved. Cook over medium heat, without stirring, to light-crack stage or to 270 degrees on candy thermometer. Pour at once on a cold, buttered marble slab. Pour oil of peppermint and food coloring on top of candy and cool slightly. Butter hands and begin pulling candy while hot. Pull until thick, then twist into rope shape and place on the marble slab. Cut with kitchen shears at once. Store in airtight container. Do not make on a rainy day.

Mrs. Katy Jo Powers, Haysi, Virginia

TAFFY

2 c. sugar	1 env. unflavored gelatin
2 c. light cream	1/3 bar paraffin
2 c. light corn syrup	1/2 tsp. vanilla

Combine the sugar, cream and syrup in a heavy saucepan and bring to a rolling boil. Soften the gelatin in 1/4 cup water and stir into sugar mixture. Add the paraffin and vanilla and cook to firm-ball stage or 246 degrees on a candy thermometer, stirring constantly. Pour on greased table top or marble slab and cool slightly. Grease hands and pull taffy. Shape into long pieces and cut into bite-sized pieces. Wrap individually in waxed paper.

Mrs. Isabel New, Tulsa, Oklahoma

PULL TAFFY

2 c. sugar   1 c. water
1 tbsp. white vinegar

Combine all ingredients in a saucepan and stir until sugar is dissolved. Cook to hard-crack stage or until mixture spins a thread. Pour out on a cold, buttered platter. Pull edges to center and centers out until cool enough to pull. Grease hands and pull candy until white and thick. Shape in rope and place on flat, greased surface. Cut into pieces.

Mrs. Edward T. Breathitt, Frankfort, Kentucky

CARAMEL CHOCOLATE SKRUNCH

2 c. corn flakes   3/4 c. dark corn syrup
1 c. crisp rice cereal   1/4 c. sugar
1/2 c. semisweet chocolate chips 2 tbsp. margarine
1 c. broken nuts   1/2 tsp. vanilla

Cut top off of 1-quart milk carton. Mix the cereals, chocolate chips and nuts in a large bowl and set aside. Mix the corn syrup, sugar and margarine in a saucepan. Bring to boil over medium heat and boil for 3 minutes, stirring constantly. Remove from heat and cool for 10 minutes. Add vanilla and beat with wooden spoon until mixture turns light brown and thickens. Pour over cereal mixture and toss to coat evenly. Pack into milk carton firmly and chill for 1 to 2 hours or until set. Cut off end of carton and down 1 side with a sharp knife and peel off carton. Cut into slices. Does not require refrigeration after loaf is set.

CARAMEL CHEWS

36 vanilla caramels
3 tbsp. light cream or
    evaporated milk
1 c. corn flakes

1 c. oven-toasted rice cereal
1 c. flaked coconut
1 c. chopped nuts

Place the caramels and cream in top of a double boiler over hot water and heat until caramels melt, stirring occasionally. Add remaining ingredients and mix quickly and thoroughly. Drop by spoonfuls on waxed paper.

Mrs. W. J. Harris, Clemson, South Carolina

CARAMEL SURPRISE CRUNCH

1/2 lb. caramels
2 tbsp. water

1/2 c. salted peanuts
7 c. corn flakes

Place the caramels and water in a double boiler and heat, stirring frequently, until caramels are melted and mixture is smooth. Add the peanuts and corn flakes and mix well. Spread on a lightly greased cookie sheet and let stand until firm. Break into pieces.

Mrs. Connie Ward, Winchester, Virginia

CEREAL BARS

1 c. light corn syrup
1 c. sugar
1 c. peanut butter
6 c. high protein cereal

1 c. flaked coconut (opt.)
1 6-oz. package chocolate
    pieces (opt.)

Place the syrup and sugar in a saucepan and heat, stirring, until bubbly. Add the peanut butter, cereal and coconut and mix well. Place in a greased 9 x 12-inch pan and sprinkle with chocolate pieces. Broil just until chocolate pieces melt and spread over cereal mixture. Cut into bars.

Mrs. N. H. Jackson, Hyattsville, Maryland

CHINESE NEW YEAR'S CANDY

1 pkg. semisweet chocolate
    pieces
1 pkg. butterscotch pieces

1 sm. can salted peanuts
1 can Chinese noodles

Place the chocolate and butterscotch pieces in top of a double boiler and melt over boiling water. Add the peanuts and noodles and mix well. Spread in a buttered pan and cool. Cut in squares and store in refrigerator.

Mrs. James E. McKenna, Norfolk, Virginia

CHOCOLATE DREAMS

1 pkg. chocolate pieces	2 1/2 c. crushed corn flakes
1 c. peanut butter	

Place the chocolate pieces and butter in a double boiler and heat until melted, stirring constantly. Add the corn flakes and mix well. Drop from teaspoon onto waxed paper and place in a cool place to harden.

Mrs. B. W. Ingram, New Castle, Delaware

CHRISTMAS PEANUT BUTTER BALLS

2 sticks butter, melted	1 1-lb. box confectioners'
1 c. chopped nuts	sugar
1 tsp. vanilla	1/2 block paraffin
1/2 c. peanut butter	1 pkg. butterscotch or
1/2 box graham crackers,	chocolate chips
crumbled	

Mix first 6 ingredients in a bowl and shape into small balls. Melt the paraffin and butterscotch chips in a double boiler. Dip the balls into butterscotch mixture and place on waxed paper to harden.

Mrs. Blanche Fletcher, Candler, North Carolina

COCOA-PEANUT BUTTER MOUNDS

2 c. sugar	3 c. quick oats
1/3 c. cocoa	1/2 c. peanut butter
1/4 c. butter	2 tsp. vanilla
1/2 c. milk	

Mix the sugar and cocoa in a saucepan. Stir in the butter and milk and bring to a boil, stirring constantly. Cook for 2 minutes and remove from heat. Stir in the oats, peanut butter and vanilla and mix well. Drop by spoonfuls onto waxed paper and cool thoroughly before serving or storing.

Mrs. Leroy Prince, Newport, Kentucky

CEREAL TREATS

1/4 c. butter	6 c. oven-toasted rice cereal
40 marshmallows	

Place the butter and marshmallows in a saucepan and cook over low heat, stirring constantly, until marshmallows are melted and mixture is smooth. Remove from heat. Add the cereal and stir until well coated. Press into a buttered pan and cool. Cut into squares.

Beverly Christiansen, Conway, Arkansas

COLD FUDGE

2 sq. chocolate	1 tsp. vanilla
2 tbsp. butter	1 1-lb. box powdered sugar
2 tbsp. peanut butter	4 to 5 tbsp. milk

Place the chocolate and butter in a saucepan and place over low heat until melted. Remove from heat. Stir in the peanut butter and vanilla and add the powdered sugar alternately with the milk. Mixture will be very stiff. Press into a pan and cut into squares.

Mrs. Mary Wooten, Chattanooga, Tennessee

OOH-OOHS

1 c. sugar	2 c. oven-toasted rice cereal
1/4 c. butter	1 tsp. vanilla
1 egg	1/2 c. chopped nuts
1 c. chopped dates	Flaked coconut

Combine the sugar, butter, egg and dates in a saucepan and mix well. Cook for 10 minutes, stirring constantly, and remove from heat. Let stand until cool enough to handle. Stir in remaining ingredients except coconut and shape into finger lengths. Roll in coconut.

Grace Hawkins, Monroe, Louisiana

ORANGE SNOWBALLS

2 3/4 c. vanilla wafer crumbs	1 c. chopped nuts
1/4 c. melted margarine	2 tbsp. soft margarine
3 c. powdered sugar	Milk
1/4 c. frozen orange juice concentrate, thawed	Shredded coconut

Mix the wafer crumbs, melted margarine, 2 cups sugar, orange concentrate and nuts in a bowl. Shape into balls. Combine the soft margarine, remaining sugar and enough milk to moisten. Dip balls in sugar mixture and roll in coconut. Store in airtight container.

Mrs. Willie Mae Cornwell, Waco, Texas

WINK'S CHEWIES

1/4 c. melted butter	1 c. raisins
1/2 lb. miniature marshmallows	1/2 c. salted peanuts or
2 sq. chocolate, melted	pecans
2 c. crushed shredded wheat	

Mix the butter, marshmallows and chocolate in a bowl. Add remaining ingredients and mix well. Spread in a buttered pan and cut in squares. Chill.

Mrs. Mary W. Winkler, West Palm Beach, Florida

WITCHES' HATS

1 oz. unsweetened chocolate	**3 c. puffed wheat cereal**
16 lge. fresh marshmallows	**1 6-oz. package chocolate**
3 tbsp. corn syrup	**pieces, melted**

Place the unsweetened chocolate, marshmallows and corn syrup in a saucepan and cook over low heat until melted, stirring constantly. Place the cereal in a shallow pan. Bake at 350 degrees, for 10 minutes, then place in a greased bowl. Pour chocolate mixture over cereal and stir to coat evenly. Shape into 8 cones and roll in melted chocolate. Cut circles out of black construction paper 1 1/2 inches larger than base of cones. Place cones, base-side down, on paper circles and cool.

Phyllis T. Smith, Lexington, Kentucky

QUICK POPCORN BALLS

1/4 c. corn oil	**1/2 c. sugar**
1/2 c. popcorn	**1/2 tsp. salt**
1/2 c. dark corn syrup	

Heat the corn oil in a 4-quart kettle over medium heat for 3 minutes. Add the popcorn and cover, leaving small air space at edge of cover. Shake frequently over medium heat until popping stops. Mix the corn syrup, sugar and salt. Add to popcorn in kettle and stir constantly over medium heat for 3 to 5 minutes or until corn is evenly and completely coated. Remove from heat and form into balls with greased hands, using as little pressure as possible. Do not double recipe. Tinted popcorn balls may be made by substituting light corn syrup for dark corn syrup, tinting syrup with desired food coloring and adding peppermint or wintergreen flavoring. 10-12 medium popcorn balls.

POPCORN BALLS

1 c. light corn syrup
1/2 c. sugar
1 3-oz. package flavored
   gelatin

1/2 lb. salted peanuts,
   coarsely chopped
9 c. popcorn

Mix the syrup and sugar in a saucepan and bring to a boil. Remove from heat. Add the gelatin and stir until dissolved. Add the peanuts. Pour over popcorn in a bowl and mix well. Shape into 1 1/2-inch balls and place on waxed paper.

Vicki Bartel, Balko, Oklahoma

PEANUT BUTTER DROPS

2 c. sugar
2 tbsp. cocoa
1 stick butter
1/2 c. cream

1/2 c. peanut butter
1 tsp. vanilla
3 c. quick oats

Combine the sugar, cocoa, butter and cream in a saucepan and bring to a boil. Cook for 1 minute. Remove from heat. Add remaining ingredients and beat until mixed. Drop from tablespoon onto waxed paper.

Mrs. Mary La Chance, Albany, Georgia

CORN FLAKE BARS

1/3 c. butter
1/2 lb. marshmallows
4 c. corn flakes
1 c. flaked coconut

1/2 c. chopped almonds
1 lge. chocolate candy bar,
   melted

Melt the butter with marshmallows in a double boiler. Add the corn flakes, coconut and almonds and mix well. Press into a greased pan and spread chocolate on top. Cool and cut into bars.

Martha Vickery, Tupelo, Mississippi

BUTTERSCOTCH PRETZELS

1 6-oz. package butterscotch
   pieces

2 tbsp. vegetable oil
12 pretzels

Melt the butterscotch pieces in oil in a double boiler, stirring frequently. Dip pretzels, one at a time, into butterscotch mixture and place on waxed paper. Chill until firm.

Mrs. L. G. Hardin, Greensboro, North Carolina

NO-COOK PEANUT BUTTER-COCONUT ROLL

1/4 c. creamy peanut butter	2 c. sifted confectioners'
1/4 c. dark corn syrup	sugar
2 tsp. water	1/4 tsp. salt
1/4 c. instant nonfat dry milk	1 c. flaked coconut, chopped

Blend the peanut butter and corn syrup in a bowl and stir in water. Sift the dry milk, confectioners' sugar and salt together and mix into peanut butter mixture. Add the coconut and knead until well blended. Shape into a roll and wrap in waxed paper. Chill for several hours or until firm. Cut into 1/4-inch slices with a sharp knife. About 3/4 pound.

Photograph for this recipe on page 156.

SMOOTH FONDANT

1/3 c. margarine	1 lb. confectioners' sugar,
1/3 c. light corn syrup	sifted
1 tsp. vanilla	3/4 lb. pitted dates
1/2 tsp. salt	Sugar

Blend the margarine, corn syrup, vanilla and salt in a large mixing bowl. Add confectioners' sugar all at once and mix with a spoon. Turn out onto a board and knead until mixture is well blended and smooth. Store in a cool place. Shape half the fondant as desired. Shape remaining fondant into very small finger-shaped rolls, stuff into dates and roll in sugar.

Photograph for this recipe on page 156.

PEANUT BUTTER CONFECTIONS

1 egg white	1 tsp. vanilla
1 1-lb. box powdered sugar	Peanut butter

Beat the egg white in a bowl until stiff. Fold in the sugar and vanilla. Roll out into an oblong shape between sheets of waxed paper. Remove waxed paper. Spread with peanut butter and roll as for jelly roll. Place in waxed paper and chill overnight. Cut into thin slices.

Alma Clayton, West End, North Carolina

TEA PARTY MINTS

1 egg white	Food coloring
1 tbsp. cream	1 1-lb. box powdered sugar
1 tsp. vanilla	2 tsp. soft butter or
3 drops of oil of peppermint	shortening

Combine the egg white, cream, vanilla, oil of peppermint and desired amount of food coloring in a bowl and stir well. Add sugar and mix thoroughly. Add the butter and additional sugar, if needed, to make firm consistency. Roll into small balls and place on waxed paper. Press each ball with tines of fork dipped in powdered sugar or cornstarch and let stand overnight. Store in covered tins with waxed paper between each layer. May be frozen.

Mrs. W. N. Bowden, Marietta, Georgia

NO-COOK MINT PATTIES

1/3 c. soft margarine	1 tsp. peppermint flavoring
1/3 c. light corn syrup	4 1/2 c. sifted powdered sugar
1/2 tsp. salt	Food coloring

Blend the margarine, corn syrup, salt and flavoring in a large mixing bowl. Add the sugar and mix until smooth. Stir in desired amount of food coloring and shape as desired. Store in cool place.

Mrs. Brendan Dixon, Charleston, South Carolina

LAZY-DAYZY NO-BAKES

1 6-oz. package semisweet chocolate morsels	1/2 c. sour cream
1 6-oz. package butterscotch-flavored morsels	1 tsp. vanilla
	1/4 tsp. salt
3/4 c. sifted confectioners' sugar	2 c. finely crushed vanilla wafer crumbs
	1/2 c. chopped toasted almonds

Combine the chocolate and butterscotch morsels in top of a double boiler and melt over hot, not boiling, water, Remove from water. Add the sugar, sour cream, vanilla and salt and mix well. Blend in the vanilla wafer crumbs and press into waxed paper-lined 8-inch square pan. Sprinkle with almonds and press in gently. Chill until firm. Let stand for several minutes at room temperature for easier cutting, then cut into 36 squares.

HONEY BALLS

1 1/2 c. instant nonfat dry
    milk
1 c. honey

1 c. peanut butter
1 can shredded coconut
1 c. whole wheat flakes

Place the milk, honey and peanut butter in a bowl and stir until thoroughly mixed. Shape into balls. Mix the coconut and wheat flakes and place on waxed paper. Roll balls in coconut mixture and chill.

Janie Haneline, Furnace, Tennessee

CHOCOLATE CHECKERS

1 c. sugar
1 c. light corn syrup
1 c. peanut butter

6 c. high protein cereal
1 lge. bag chocolate pieces,
    melted

Combine the sugar and syrup in a saucepan and bring to a boil over moderate heat, stirring frequently. Remove from heat. Stir in the peanut butter and cereal and blend well. Press into a buttered 13 x 9-inch pan and top with chocolate. Cool and cut into squares.

Mrs. F. R. Ross, Jacksonville, Alabama

CHOCOLATE-MARSHMALLOW BARS

1 6-oz. package chocolate
    pieces
1 6-oz. package butterscotch
    pieces

3/4 c. peanut butter
2 c. miniature marshmallows
1 c. chopped walnuts

Mix the chocolate, butterscotch and peanut butter in top of double boiler and place over boiling water until melted. Mix in marshmallows and walnuts. Press into an 8 x 8-inch buttered pan and chill. Cut into bars.

Carol North, Crestview, Florida

POPCORN CONFECTION

1 c. (packed) brown sugar
1 c. sugar
3/4 c. sugar

6 tbsp. butter
3 tbsp. light corn syrup
4 qt. popcorn

Mix all ingredients except popcorn in a large saucepan and cook to hard-ball stage. Pour over popcorn and stir until all popcorn is coated. Place in a greased cookie pan and cool. Separate popcorn.

Peppy Young, Hugo, Oklahoma

TEXAS PECAN PRALINES

1 1/2 c. (firmly packed) brown
   sugar
1 1/2 c. sugar

1/4 c. butter
1 c. heavy cream
2 c. pecan halves

Combine the sugars, butter and cream in a saucepan and blend thoroughly. Bring to a boil, stirring until sugar is dissolved, then cook to soft-ball stage, stirring occasionally. Add the pecans and beat until thickened. Drop by tablespoonfuls onto waxed paper, having at least 3 pecan halves in each praline. Let stand until firm, then remove from waxed paper carefully.

Mrs. L. D. Anderson, Crosbyton, Texas

MAGIC PENUCHE LOG

1 1/4 c. sugar
3/4 c. (firmly-packed) brown
   sugar
1/4 tsp. salt
2/3 c. milk

7 tbsp. butter or margarine
1 tsp. vanilla
3/4 c. coarsely chopped walnuts
4 c. puffed wheat
3 c. miniature marshmallows

Combine the sugars, salt and milk in a saucepan and cook over low heat until sugars dissolve, stirring occasionally. Cook, without stirring, to soft-ball stage or 236 degrees on candy thermometer. Remove from heat and add 4 tablespoons butter and vanilla. Do not stir. Cool at room temperature to warm or 110 degrees without stirring. Beat vigorously until mixture is thick and loses gloss. Stir in the walnuts and shape into roll about 10 inches long. Wrap in waxed paper and refrigerate for about 2 hours or until firm. Place the puffed wheat in a shallow baking pan. Bake at 350 degrees for about 10 minutes, then pour into a large, greased bowl. Melt remaining butter and marshmallows in a saucepan over low heat, stirring occasionally. Pour over puffed wheat and stir until evenly coated. Shape evenly around penuche roll with greased hands to form a log. Refrigerate for about 1 hour, then slice.

MEXICAN PECAN CANDY

2 c. sugar
3/4 c. milk
1/2 tsp. soda

1 tsp. vanilla
1 c. chopped pecans

Mix the sugar and milk in a saucepan and stir in the soda. Cook over low heat to soft-ball stage and remove from heat. Add the vanilla and pecans and beat until creamy. Drop by teaspoonfuls onto waxed paper.

Mrs. J. L. Mitchell, San Antonio, Texas

STRAWBERRY CANDIES

5 3-oz. packages strawberry
   gelatin
2 c. flaked coconut
2 c. ground pecans

1 can sweetened condensed milk
1/3 c. sugar
Red food coloring

Mix the gelatin, coconut, pecans and milk in a bowl and let stand for about 20 minutes. Shape into strawberries. Mix the sugar with several drops of food coloring and roll each strawberry in colored sugar. Garnish each strawberry with 2 nandina leaves.

Mrs. M. M. Erion, Little Rock, Arkansas

CHOCOLATE OVER NUTS

4 1/2 c. sugar
1 lge. can evaporated milk
2 sticks butter or margarine

3 6-oz. packages chocolate pieces
1 1/2 tsp. vanilla
2 c. broken nuts

Mix the sugar and milk in a saucepan and bring to a boil. Cook, stirring constantly, for 10 minutes. Add the butter and chocolate and stir until melted. Stir in the vanilla and nuts and place in an oblong pan. Cool. Cut in squares.

June Elizabeth Rector, Abingdon, Virginia

SUGARED NUTS

1 1/2 c. sugar
1/2 c. sour cream
2 tbsp. butter

1 tsp. vanilla
1 tsp. cinnamon
2 1/2 c. chopped walnuts

Mix the sugar, sour cream and butter in a heavy saucepan and bring to a boil. Cook over low heat to soft-ball stage or 238 degrees on a candy thermometer, stirring frequently. Cool. Add the vanilla and cinnamon and stir in walnuts. Drop from spoon onto buttered foil.

Mrs. Bob Crenshaw, Santa Fe, New Mexico

INDEX

191

PHOTOGRAPHY CREDITS: Kellogg Company; The Nestle Company; American Dairy Association; Best Foods: A Division of CPC International, Incorporated; Quaker Oats; C & H Sugar Kitchen; Pet, Incorporated; Grandma's West Indies Molasses; United Fresh Fruit and Vegetable Association; Cling Peach Advisory Board; Evaporated Milk Association; National Peanut Council; Angostura-Wuppermann Corporation; North American Blueberry Council; Peter Pan Peanut Butter; Procter & Gamble Company; California Raisin Advisory Board; Diamond Walnut Growers, Incorporated; Keith Thomas Company; National Dairy Council; Processed Apples Institute; Ocean Spray Cranberries; Dried Fig Advisory Board.

Printed in the United States of America.